ACOUSTIC GUITAR FOR BEGINNERS

The Complete Idiot's Guide to Acoustic Guitar, Covering Everything There Is to Know (2022 Crash Course for Newbies)

Mia Walkeins

TABLE OF CONTENTS

Introduction

The acoustic guitar is one of the best types of guitar to start with as a beginner. The presence of a sound box, which amplifies the sound of the strings, distinguishes an acoustic guitar. An acoustic guitar does not require an amplifier or speakers to produce a strong sound. As a result, you can easily pick up an acoustic guitar and practice wherever you want.

Acoustic guitars have a soulful and beautiful sound, making them versatile instruments that can be used in a variety of music genres. So, learning to play an acoustic guitar could be one of the coolest instruments you learn this year. The guitar, as we know it, is at least a century old, and its roots as a stringed instrument go back even further.

Many folk instruments have used the same basic design for thousands of years, with strings stretched across the fretboard and plucked with the fingers. In some ways, the guitar is the culmination of that legacy, which explains its versatility. If you enjoy playing the guitar, this book will come in handy. Regardless of your background, situation, or motivations, the goal of this book is to provide you with enough information to allow you to explore everything on your own.

It's common for beginners to feel stuck at a certain point in their guitar learning. We will enlighten you with exceptional methods that will accelerate your learning curve with this beginner's guide. Understanding what you can do with the guitar, discovering new ways to make new sounds, and gaining a better understanding of how to fret notes and chords that seemed impossible before becomes exhilarating and satisfying. All of this is available to you if you are willing to invest some time and effort in understanding everything this book has to offer. We make no assumptions about your ability to play the guitar or read music.

So, for you to understand everything about playing the guitar from the ground up. To make comprehension easier, we begin this guide with the fundamentals. And with the straightforward, informal explanation of how guitars work, the various types of guitars, and how to play, form chords, strum, and fingerpick strings, you can broaden your knowledge in a variety of directions. Without further ado, let us begin with guitar history and progress to something more advanced.

Chapter 1

Guitar History and Types

To begin this beginner's guide to learning how to play an acoustic guitar, let's go back in time to the history of guitars. We believe it is especially important to discuss this first because it is always best to know where it all started. Guitars are widely used in folk and popular music in many countries, which has resulted in the numerous origin stories we all hear when we ask where the guitar was born.

Depending on who you ask, the origins of the guitar range from Persia to Greece. Perhaps it was born in this region, but variations of strings and plucked instruments can be found all over the world, demonstrating ingenuity and creativity that transcends culture.

The Guitar's History

The guitar is a string instrument that dates back to the early 16th century in Spain. The guitar, as we know it today, is a descendant of the late-medieval instrument Guitarra Latina. The Latina Guitarra is a four-string instrument. The first guitars had a less pronounced waist, were narrower and deeper, and were smaller in size. Guitarra Latina is closely related to the Vihuela in many ways. Vihuela is a guitar-like instrument that is commonly used in Spain instead of the lute. Previously, guitars only had four strings: three doubles and a single top string. As with the violin peg-box, the strings were glued and stretched from the tension bridge to the soundboard or belly of the guitar. The bridge keeps the direct pull of the strings going. A circular sound hole in the belly of the guitar is also common, often adorned with a carved wooden rose.

The majority of modern guitar advancements occurred between the 16th and 19th centuries. Guitar strings were tuned to sound C-F-A-D apart in the 16th century, similar to how the center four courses of the Vihuela and the Lute were tuned. A fifth string was added to the guitar before 1600, and a sixth string was added in the late 18th century. Around the year 1800, music innovators replaced the guitar's double strings with a single string, tuning the guitar to E-A-D-G-B-E, which has remained the standard tuning for the guitar to this day.

Another improvement made to the guitar around 1600 was the replacement of the violin-styled peg-box with a flat and slightly reflexed head with rear tuning pegs. Later, in the nineteenth century, inventors devised metal screws to replace the tuning pegs.

Previously, the frets were tied to the guitar's gut, but in the 18th century, they were replaced with ivory or metal frets. The fingerboard was originally flush with the belly and ended there, with some ivory or metal frets on the belly. Later in the nineteenth century, the fingerboard was improved by raising it to a level higher than the belly, causing it to extend across the edge of the sound hole.

Furthermore, in the nineteenth century, the guitar's body underwent a few changes that improved the instrument's sonority. This enhancement resulted in the guitar becoming wider and shallower, with an extremely thin soundboard. Similarly, the transverse bars that reinforce the soundboard were replaced with radial bars that fan out below the sound hole. In addition, the neck of the guitar forms a brace or shoe that projects a short distance inside the body of the guitar and is glued to the back. This advancement strengthened the guitar's resistance to string pull.

So there's no denying that the guitar or instruments related to the guitar have been around since ancient times. The concept of a stretched string vibrating over a chamber of air known as the sound box is not novel. This concept dates back to prehistoric times and has been adopted by many cultures around the world. The use of frets to mark tones to scale the sound was most likely invented in India. Later, early explorers from Portugal and Spain most likely introduced the guitar to Europe, and European settlers introduced it to America.

Most of the innovations seen on the guitar in the nineteenth century were the brainchild of Antonio Torres, the most important Spanish guitar maker. Most acoustic guitars on the market today are based on their design. His design resulted in the classical guitar, which is strung with three metal-spun silk and three gut strings. As technology advanced, manufacturers began to substitute plastic and nylon strings for the gut. The 12-stringed or double-course guitar, Mexican Jarana, and South America Charango (both of which are five-course guitars) were all strung with nylon or plastic strings. Lyreshaped guitars were the most popular in the nineteenth century. However, other types of guitar exist, such as metal-stringed guitars used in folk and popular music, cello guitars with tailpieces, and violin-styled bridges. Other types of guitars include the Hawaiian or steel-strung guitar, which has strings that are stopped by the pressure of a metal bar, producing a sweet gliding tone, and the electric guitar. Guitar Styles

Today, there are so many different types of guitars that it almost seems impossible to keep up. Even more frustrating is the fact that acoustic guitars can look very similar. And because acoustic guitars are made of wood, they all have a sound hole and strings, so there is no obvious distinguishing feature. However, guitars are primarily classified based on the strings used, body shape, and tone wood design. So, to help you understand better, here's a rundown of the various types of acoustic guitars and what genre to use them for, as well as some features you'll appreciate.

1. Guitar Dreadnought

Dreadnought guitars are a popular type of guitar on the market today. The dreadnought guitar is still the most affordable of the various types of guitars available today. C.F. Martin & Company, an American guitar manufacturer, invented them in the twentieth century. The term "dreadnought guitar" comes from the name of the large, all-big-gun modern battleship HMS Dreadnought. It has a large body that produces a bolder, louder, and richer tone. The dreadnought guitar is distinguished by its size, square shoulder, and bottom. Furthermore, the neck of a dreadnought guitar is typically joined to the body at the fourteenth fret.

The D-sized guitar, or simply dreads among guitarists, is another name for the C.F. Martin & Company dreadnought guitar.

C.F. Martin & Company dreadnought guitar model numbers begin with a D followed by a number, such as D-18 or D-45. It is important to note that the higher the number assigned to the model number, the more decoration, and ornamentation on the guitar. Dreadnought guitars are ideal for aggressive strummers and flat pickers looking for a powerful but affordable instrument. Dreadnought guitars are commonly used by blues guitarists.

2. Giant Guitar

The jumbo guitar, popularized by Gibson in the 1930s, is another popular type of guitar among guitarists. The jumbo guitar has a more curved centric design than the dreadnought guitar. Jumbo guitars are distinguished by their relatively large sound box, which produces the most air inside the body, resulting in more energy coming out of them. Jumbo guitars typically have a circular body shape with a tight waist that gives them a snappy top end and presence. The jumbo guitar's tighter waist prevents it from losing clarity or sounding muddy.

The jumbo guitar is not recommended for fingerpicking or gentle players, but it is the ultimate strummer's guitar.

Jumbo guitars are frequently used in popular folk, pop, and country songs.

Furthermore, the jumbo acoustic guitar's tonal spectrum is well-balanced. I can tell you from personal experience that the larger cavity produces a more open type of sound that can accentuate the bass frequencies. The Jumbo guitar is used by famous guitarists such as George Harrison and Elvis Presley.

3. Guitar for the Parlor

This parlor acoustic guitar sits on the other end of the shape. This guitar is among the smallest in body size that you can buy, not including modern baby guitars. Parlor guitars are preferred by musicians who prefer a more low-key, less brash musical style, such as indie and folk. The distinctive body shape of this guitar, once again from C.F Martin & Company, is joined to the body on the 12th fret.

The shoulder where the body meets the neck is slightly steeper than in dreadnought acoustic guitars. At the same time, the base of a guitar's body will be narrower than that of a larger guitar. Finally, the goal is to make it more comfortable to play and to create a less physically demanding playing experience.

Parlor guitars are associated with the renowned guitarist Ian Anderson in terms of precedent

4. Rounded Shoulders Dreadnought Guitar

After we've gone over the three main shapes of steel-stung acoustic guitar - the dreadnought, jumbo, and parlor guitar - let's look at the offshoots and variants. The rounded shoulder dreadnought guitar is the first in this category.

This is a well-known and recognizable Gibson creation, as used by Noel Gallagher and the Beatles. Because of its sweet, warm, and beautifully defined mid-range high notes, the rounded shoulder dreadnought guitar is difficult to overlook.

The rounded shoulder dreadnought guitar evolved from replication of Martin's dreadnought guitar. Gibson designed a slight variation on the dreadnought that became extremely popular.

After its popularity grew, it was dubbed a "workhorse" guitar because it was less expensive and easier to maintain than the more expensive dreadnought. The rounded shoulders dreadnought's price contributed to its rise to prominence, as did its warm tone, which offers a luscious sound that complements any vocalist in the acoustic arena.

5. Guitars for Auditoriums

Auditorium guitars are similar to dreadnought guitars, but their development history is more recent. This type of guitar is yet another C.F. Martin house design. While this guitar has a similar dimension to the dreadnought. However, a closer examination of the auditorium guitar reveals that it has a much tighter waist, which can cause certain tonal characteristics to become much more pronounced. Because of its refined waist, the auditorium guitar fits over your leg more snugly.

The inner curves of the body on the auditorium guitar have been defined more inward, reducing the amount of inner cavity of the guitar shape. This feature is especially useful for players who prefer to have their guitar sit firmly on their legs without moving around. Eric Clapton is a well-known guitarist who includes the auditorium guitar in his repertoire. If you've heard his "unplugged" album, you'll recognize the lovely tones that can emerge from the auditorium guitar.

6. Concert Guitar

Another type of acoustic guitar that differs in tone and functionality is the concert guitar. Concert guitars sound more pleasing and playable overall. Aside from that, concert guitars are small in comparison to larger guitars such as dreadnought guitars. Even though concert guitars lack volume, manufacturers compensate with articulating tones that are more prominent in the upper and middle ranges.

Take note that the size and shape of a guitar affect not only the sound but also how it plays. As a result, the small compact nature of concert guitars makes them very comfortable to play for smaller people.

Guitarists who enjoy the sound of fingerpicking will appreciate the concert guitar's lower string tension. Furthermore, the articulate tone of concert guitars makes them ideal for fingerpicking. Remember that there are no hard and fast rules about who can and cannot play the concert guitar. So, if you enjoy the positive aspects of the guitar, don't let anything stop you.

7. Guitar Classical

Classical guitar is another type of guide known for its soft nylon-string tone, though they can also be strung with steel strings for a unique sound. The open-slotted tuners on classical guitars are one of the easiest ways to identify them. Cams, rather than standard tuning posts, are used in slotted tuners. Tuner knobs frequently recede perpendicularly from the back of the headstock rather than parallel with the side of the headstock. The well-known Spanish guitar is an example of a classical guitar.

If you enjoy fingerpicking or soft sounds, particularly from European orchestral music, the classical guitar is an excellent investment. Similarly, if you enjoy strumming, classical guitars can easily become a good strummer. Willie Nelson, Andres Segovia, and Christopher Parkening are among the famous guitarists associated with classical guitar.

8. Travel Guitar

Travel guitars, as the name suggests, are ideal for players who travel frequently or have small hands. Because of its extremely compact design, parents frequently shop for this type of guitar for their children.

This guitar was created to provide comfort and convenience for a small player while traveling. One of the major issues with smaller guitars is that sound quality suffers as a result. As a result, music manufacturers invested significant time and resources in developing the ideal small-scale acoustic guitar, giving rise to the travel guitar.

While they are small and cute, they are not toys; most of them have a full-size fretboard, or something close to a full-size fretboard, of around 23 inches in length and provide a very similar playing experience to a full-sized guitar. They may even cost more than a standard acoustic guitar in some cases. Most travel guitars are made of laminated wood to ensure humidity and temperature resistance while remaining lightweight. 9. Flamenco Guitar

Finally, the flamenco guitar is similar to the classical guitar, but it has a thinner top and less internal bracing.

Because of their thinner top, flamenco guitars produce a brighter and more percussive sound. Most flamenco guitars use nylon strings rather than steel strings, giving them a more lively sound when compared to classical guitars. Flamenco guitar volume is critical to guitarists because it is heard over the sound of the dancers' nailed shoes. When making a flamenco guitar, guitar makers primarily use hardwoods such as rosewood for the back and sides and softer woods for the top.

A well-constructed flamenco guitar responds faster and has less sustenance than classical guitars. Flamenco guitars are desirable for this feature because a good flamenco player's fury of notes may sound muddy on a guitar with a lush, sustained, big sound. Flamenco guitars are also often described as percussive, with a drier, brighter, and more austere sound.

Chapter 2

Anatomy of a Guitar,

In addition to everything covered in the first chapter, the goal of this chapter is to introduce you to the guitar in greater depth. In this chapter, we'll look at the various parts of the guitar and the functions they serve. By the end of this chapter, you will know the names of each guitar part, so that when we discuss how to buy a guitar in the next chapter, you will not be confused.

The Structure of a Guitar

There are two kinds of guitars: electric and acoustic. There are several subdivisions within each of these basic types of guitar.

Because the acoustic guitar is the focus of this book, we will concentrate on the various components that comprise an acoustic guitar.

Making an electric guitar is generally easier than making an acoustic guitar, according to guitar manufacturers. As a result, the acoustic guitar is frequently more expensive. A lot of precision is required when putting together an acoustic guitar, especially with the sound box.

As seen in the image above, the acoustic guitar is divided into three major sections: the headstock, neck, and body.

You'll find various parts of the guitar in these sections that work together to produce a beautiful sound.

1. The headstock

The mechanism that secures the strings to the head of the guitar is located on the headstock. The tuners are located on the headstock. Many manufacturers inscribe their logo on the headstock. There are two traditional headstock designs available on the market.

Guitars are available in two configurations: 3+3, which means three tuners on top and three on the bottom, or 6 with six tuners on top of the headstock. Furthermore, your guitar's headstock can be straight or carved separately and glued to the neck. • Tweakers

The tuner, also known as the tuning machine, tuning keys, tuning gears, or tuning pegs, is an important component of a guitar. The tuner on an acoustic or electric guitar is usually located on the headstock. The tuners are a geared mechanism that is in charge of tuning the guitar. Tuning a guitar with tuners involves either rotating the tuners or wrapping the string around the post of the tuner. Depending on which direction you rotate the tuner, you may be tightening or loosening the strings. The higher the pitch of the string, the tighter the string tension.

• Nut The nut acts as a link between the headstock and the neck of the guitar. The nut has grooves on it that serve as a demarcation, separating the strings as you tighten them to pitch. The nut can be made of a variety of materials, including stiff nylon, silver, bone, brass, or other synthetic materials. When the strings vibrate, the nut prevents them from vibrating past the neck. The nut is one of two points on the guitar where the vibrating area of the string ends; the other point is the bridge, which is located on the guitar's body.

2. Neck

The neck of a guitar is the club-like, long section of the guitar that connects the body and the headstock. The neck of a guitar is usually made of hardwood. The fingerboard and fretboard are frequently made of the same wood, while the neck is made of different wood. A guitar's neck must be rigid and resistant to bending, even when using high tension strings. The rigidity of a guitar's neck can be used to determine its quality.

It should be noted that the guitar's neck, which houses the fingerboard and frets, is an integral part of the instrument. This is where you hold the strings at various sections of the fingerboards to vary the pitch of the strings and produce a lovely sound.

fingerboard

Because the frets are embedded in the fingerboard, it is also known as the fretboard. The fingerboard is a plank-like piece of wood that is often laminated and sits on the guitar's neck. It is an essential part of the guitar because it is where your finger is placed.

Strings are typically run across the fingerboard between the bridge and nut. When you play the guitar, every time you depress a string on the fingerboard, you change the length of the string, and thus the pitch. You can even play notes using only your fretting hands by hammering on the string.

• Frets

Every guitar has frets located on the fingerboard. Frets can be made of wire or a thin bar that runs parallel to the strings. The frets span the entire width of the neck, with varying spacing between each fret. The shorter the distance between the frets, the closer you get to the body. Furthermore, the fretboard is in charge of shortening the vibrating length of the string, allowing you to produce different pitches. In the standard Western system, an octave is divided into twelve semitones, so each fret on the guitar represents a semitone.

• Marker of Position

Position markers are single or double dots inlaid on the fretboard or the edge of the guitar's neck to aid in fret navigation. You don't always have to count the frets as a beginner learning to play the guitar to know how many you're playing on.

The single dot position markers are commonly used on the third, fifth, seventh, and ninth frets of the guitar. Position markers are placed high above the neck on the 12th and 24th frets to indicate an octave higher double dot. This position marker can be illuminated with light diodes to make it more visible on stage.

3. Body

Moving on, the body of a guitar is the large box on the instrument. The body serves as a foundation for the neck and bridge, as well as a surface for your right hand to strum over the strings. The body contains an amplifying sound chamber, which allows the guitar to produce a more pronounced tone. The body of the guitar is the curvy part that rests against your body while playing. Take note that the body of the guitar can vary in shape. Some guitars have a cut-out near the neck that allows you to easily reach the frets above the neck.

• Sound Gap

The sound hole is the round opening on the body of a guitar.

The sound is amplified when strings vibrate over the sound hole. The sound hole on some acoustic guitars is usually oval.

Although the sound hole on an acoustic guitar amplifies and improves the sound, this does not imply that the sound comes solely from the sound hole. The surface of the sounding boards also generates sounds. The sound hole only serves as an entrance to the resonant chamber formed by the body.

The pickguard is another component of the guitar's body.

The pickguard does not contribute to the sound of the guitar. The pickguard, on the other hand, protects the finish of your guitar from scratches. If the pickguard is in place, the pick will not scratch the finish of the guitar while playing. The pickguard is typically made of plastic or another material that has been laminated. Another function of the pickguard is decoration, as it is frequently made of a color that contrasts with the color of the guitar body. Luxury pickguards on high-end guitars may be made of furs, exotic woods, gems, skins, or precious metal.

• A span

The bridge of a guitar is the part of the body that holds the strings in place. So, on any guitar, the string runs from the bridge to the tuner on the headstock. The bridge of a guitar is typically placed perpendicular to the strings on the body and securely glued so that it can support the tension of the strings. To withstand such tension, the bridge is frequently made of high-density plastic, metal, ivory, or bone. The bridge is made up of several parts, including the bridge pin and a separate bearing surface known as the saddle.

The bridge pin, also known as string pegs, is used to keep the string in place. Bridge pins are used on the majority of steel-stringed acoustic guitars. Bridge pins for guitars can be made of brass, bone, ivory, wood, or even plastic. It's worth noting that not all acoustic guitars use bridge pins; it all depends on the bridge's design. Some guitar manufacturers designed their bridges so that when it comes to fastening strings, you simply pass them through the bridge's holes, and the string ball at the end of the string keeps the string from going through the bridge's hole.

• Saddlecloth

The saddle is another component of the guitar that can be found on the bridge. The saddle influences the overall height of the strings above the fretboard. The closer the strings are to the fretboard, the easier it will be to hold chords with your left hand.

As a result, the saddle has a greater impact on the playability and tone of the guitar than you might think. There are two types of saddles: compensated saddles and uncompensated saddles. Notches or grooves in compensated saddles are where the high E, B, and G strings rest.

As a result, the length of the string is adjusted, compensating for accurate intonation. The uncompensated saddle, on the other hand, has no grooves and is flat across the surface.

• Pin at the end

The endpin is a metal post at the back of the guitar body to which the strap can be attached. The Pin contains the output hack for routing signals from the guitar's preamp and pickup in some acoustic-electric guitars with built-in electronics and pickups.

four. strings

The last one is the string, which is a vital part of the guitar that produces the sound. When the strings are plucked, they vibrate, producing sounds that are amplified in the sound box. A guitar string runs from the bridge to the tuner on the headstock. To achieve the desired sound, you can use various types of strings on your guitar. Nylon string and metal string are the two most common types of strings.

The Operation of a Guitar

Now that we've established the fundamental components of the guitar, we'll look at how they all work together to produce sound.

The primary goal of this section will be to learn how to play the guitar.

We'll talk about the strings, plucking the strings, and how the frets affect the sound you make.

1. Vibration and Length of String

The guitar makes sound by vibrating its strings over a sound box. An acoustic guitar has six strings, as we established in the previous chapter. However, these strings must be brought to a certain tension. A tuned string gets its name from the note it produces when plucked open. The A string is so named because playing the A string open produces an A note. However, you can change the note by changing the length of the string by fretting it. As a result, you can produce something melodious by varying the length of the strings.

2. Using Your Left and Right Hands

To play the guitar, you need your left hand fretting the string and your right hand plucking the string, as we just established.

When you hold a note or a chord on a guitar with your left hand, your right hand is in charge of plucking or strumming the string to produce the sound of the note or chord you are holding. Later in this book, we'll go over how to play notes and chords on the guitar in detail.

3. A fret is half a step.

A half-step is a distance between two frets on a guitar. To move a full step, you must move two frets on the guitar. To play an octave on the guitar, you must move 12 frets rather than 6 frets.

4. Collections

The sound of a vibrating string must be amplified; otherwise, it will be too quiet. You won't have any trouble with an acoustic guitar because the hollow sound chamber amplifies the sound.

The way you control the pitches on a guitar determines how different it sounds from the sound you envision. Your left hand is for fretting, which you'll use to change the pitches, and your right hand is for producing the sound and determining the rhythm, tempo, and feel of those pitches. Putting both hands to work equals guitar music.

One of the most difficult aspects of learning to play any musical instrument is gaining a thorough understanding of the instrument. The tedious process of tuning the guitar can be quite difficult. Fortunately for guitarists, unlike the piano, the guitar only has six strings. However, before you begin tuning the guitar, you must first understand how to refer to the two main parts of the instrument: frets and strings.

1. a string

As previously stated, a guitar has six strings labeled 1 through 6. When holding the guitar in a playing position, the first string is the thinnest and closest to the floor. Moving up, the 6th string is the fattest and closest to the ceiling when holding the guitar in a playing position. The string numbering on a guitar may appear counterintuitive because, when holding the guitar in a playing position, the first string you see is what you may want to call the first string, but it is the 6th string. The strings are labeled E, B, G, D, A, and E from the first to the sixth.

2. Frets

The frets, which indicate the spaces where you place your left-hand fingers to vary the length of the strings to change the pitch of the guitar, should also be labeled. The first fret is closest to the nut.

Likewise, the fifth fret is the area between the fourth and fifth metal bars. Many guitars have 5th fret markers, which can be a dot or a decorative design embedded in the fretboard.

Purchasing and Stringing a Guitar

If you don't already own a guitar, you should get one. This chapter will teach you how to choose the best guitar. Remember that the entire process of purchasing a guitar is exciting and tantalizing. When you indulge yourself, you can tell the difference between a good guitar and a great guitar. Play a variety of guitars to learn the distinctions between high-quality, expensive, and acceptable but affordable guitars.

Creating a Purchasing Strategy

The first step in attempting to purchase a guitar is to devise a purchasing strategy. In this section, you must ask yourself a series of questions and honestly answer them. Remember, there are no correct or incorrect answers. You should not wait until you are in the store to begin developing a purchasing strategy.

When developing a buying strategy, the two most important things to remember are to create a plan and to gather all of the necessary information. So, consider the following questions:

1. What is my level of dedication?

Aside from your current playing ability, do you see yourself practicing the guitar every day for the next five years? Or do you see yourself just trying out the guitar to try new things and hoping it sticks? If the latter is the case, spending a lot of money on a high-quality guitar will go a long way. However, if the latter is the case, it is not advisable to spend too much money on a guitar, at least not until you are certain of its importance in your life. Importantly, when purchasing a guitar, spend responsibly and according to your priorities.

2. What is my financial limit?

Another critical question you must ask yourself is how much money you are willing to spend. The more expensive the guitar, the more appealing it is. So, if you follow your instincts, you may end up spending more than you can afford. You must strike a balance between your level of commitment and the amount available. Set a spending limit for yourself and stick to it.

3. Should I shop online or in a mall?

If you have everything planned out, right down to the color and options you want, you can consider purchasing the guitar from an online vendor. However, if you are still unsure about the guitar you want to buy, you should go to a mall to buy one.

You can even try out the guitar at the mall before purchasing it. Furthermore, when purchasing a guitar at a mall, you can get the best deals and even avoid paying sales tax, especially if the music company is located out of state.

4. Is it better to buy a new or used guitar?

Which personality type are you? If you want to buy a used guitar, keep in mind that vintage instruments can be quite expensive, but they provide a unique experience when played. However, if you are on a tight budget, there are other less expensive used guitars you can purchase.

Not to mention the benefits of new guitars that used guitars may not have. If, on the other hand, you prefer the sensation of playing a brand-new guitar and can afford to buy one, go ahead.

Look for stores that provide discounts at various rates.

Determine Your Needs for a Guitar

Knowing what you can afford to spend on a guitar is an important buyer's guide feature to think about. A budget categorizes products and gives you an idea of what you are likely to purchase. For example, if one person has a $1000 budget and another has a $200 budget, you can't expect the person with the $200 budget to get a better guitar than the person with the $1000 budget. The quality you receive is influenced by your budget. Your budget has an impact on the following factors.

1. Physical appearance

The aesthetic properties of your guitar are related to its appearance. The nice wood finishing and color all play a role here. When you like the way your guitar looks, you're more likely to pick it up for practice. Feel free to base your decision on the appearance of the guitar you want to buy. A green guitar is not superior to a red guitar.

2. Adaptability

Some guitars are easier to play than others, and it is important to keep this in mind when purchasing a guitar. Because of the less craftsmanship used during construction, cheaper guitars are frequently more difficult to play. It is common for cheap guitars to have strings that are far from the fret. As a result, depressing the string to the fretboard will be difficult.

3. Accentuation

A good guitar must be in tune. To test a guitar's intonation, play the 12th fret harmonic (barely touching the fret rather than pressing it down) on the first string and match it to the fretted note at the 12th fret. Although the pitch is the same, the notes have different tonal qualities. Use the same test on all six strings of the guitar, paying special attention to the third and sixth strings. Typically, the third and sixth strings are the first to go out of tune.

4. Solid Construction

Finally, your budget will determine the type of construction used on the guitar you want to buy. Examine every joint for sloppy workmanship when inspecting a well-built guitar. A rough-sanded brace is a dead giveaway that the guitar was thrown together quickly.

Purchasing a Guitar To get started on the right foot, you must first decide how much money you are willing to spend. A large budget does not guarantee that you will get the best guitar. If you want to get the best guitar, you must keep certain characteristics in mind. Here's a rundown of everything you should be on the lookout for:

1. Development

When we talk about guitar construction, we mean how it is designed and assembled. The construction of a guitar defines the guitar and the type of music it can easily play. The three most important issues concerning guitar construction are listed below.

Laminated Wood vs. Solid Wood

The guitar's quality ranges from solid wood to laminated wood. To be honest, a solid wood guitar is more likely to last than a laminated wood guitar. Regardless, most manufacturers use several layers of cheap wood, pressed together and veneered, which will not last long. Guitars made of solid wood are more durable, but their prices can reach $1000.

The type of wood used in guitars is an important factor in sound production. When a guitar string is plucked, the sound vibrates in the sound box, striking the back and sides before reflecting through the sound hole. A hardwood guitar is a good choice, but it's worth considering different configurations, such as the top being solid and various parts being laminated, to cut costs. A guitar with a solid top but laminated back and sides, which costs around $400, is a good option.

Whether or not the guitar you want to buy has a cap is another determining factor of quality. This feature also reflects the guitar's price. The cap serves as a layer of fine decorative wood, usually figured maple. Other popular woods used by manufacturers include quilted and flame maple. Figured wood tops are also used when manufacturers want to make a guitar with a clear finish to show off the wood's attractive grain pattern.

Neck Structure

Here are the three most common types of neck construction, in order of cost, from least expensive to most expensive:

• Attachment

Some guitars are made with bolt-on construction. The neck of this guitar is bolted to the back of the guitar at the heel with 4 or 5 bolts. However, the heel plates may occasionally cover the bolt holes.

• Set-In (or Glued-In)

Another common guitar construction is the neck and body being joined in an unbroken surface covering connection. This style of construction creates a seamless effect from the body to the neck, and the joints are glued together. • Body-Through-Neck

Another common type of construction found in high-quality guitars is one in which the neck and headstock are one long unit. Although the guitar has a single long neck, it also has several wood pieces glued to it. But it doesn't stop there; it continues to the tail of the guitar.

2. Material

While the material used to construct a guitar is important, you should not base the guitar's durability solely on the material used in its construction. Consider a guitar made of higher-quality materials, which will last longer and stand the test of time.

- **Wood**

Wood is the most commonly used material in the construction of guitars. When manufacturers use expensive or rare wood to build a guitar, the price will rise. We can divide the quality of wood used in guitar construction into three categories:

• Types

The first criterion we will investigate is the type of wood used.

Mahogany, maple, and rosewood are some of the woods that have been used. Rosewood is the most popular hardwood used in guitar construction, but it is also the most expensive, followed by maple and then mahogany.

• Style

We can also classify the type of wood used in the guitar's construction by examining the wood's region and grain styles. Brazilian rosewood is darker and more grainy than East Indian rosewood, but it is more expensive. Flame and quilted maples are more expensive than bird's-eye or rock maples.

• Grade

Finally, guitar manufacturers use a grading system ranging from A to AA (the highest) to assess the wood's grade, color, and consistency. A high-quality guitar is made from high-quality wood.

3. Bridge and Tuner Assemblies

In most expensive instruments, components, including hardware, can be easily upgraded. However, there are only a few guitar upgrades available, such as the bridge assembly and tuner. You can upgrade your tuner from chrome-plated to something more luster, such as gold-plated or black-matte. Similarly, you can improve the bridge assembly, knobs, and switches, among other things.

4. Craftsmanship

When purchasing expensive guitars, the craftsmanship that went into the construction must be more than perfectly fine. You can inspect the interior of the acoustic guitar to ensure that there are no complicated constructions inside. It's only natural to find a few gapless joints in acoustic guitars under $600. In essence, playing an expensive guitar should be a pleasurable experience.

Guitar Stringing

When it comes to stringing a guitar, you can use either steel or nylon strings. The steps below will show you how to change the strings and tune them.

Steel string guitar stringing

Stringing a steel string on an acoustic guitar can be difficult. There are two main steps to changing or restringing your guitar. The first step is to tie the string to the bridge. The strings should then be attached to the tuner, which can be used to tighten the string tension.

Step 1: Connect the String to the Bridge

1. Pry up the bridge pin with a needle-nose plier.

2. Insert the end of the new string (called the ball or string ring) into the role where the bridge pin was removed.

3. Firmly wedge the bridge pin. Place the bridge pin so that the bridge slot is facing the nut.

4. Gently pull the string until the ball rests against the bridge pin's bottom.

5. Gently tug on the string to test it

Step 2: Attach the String to the Tuners

1. Thread the string through the post's hole.

2. Bend the metal wire in the direction of the guitar.

3. Tighten the string to the post by rotating the peg clockwise.

Nylon-String Guitar Stringing

The nylon string is another common type of string that is quite different from stringing a steel-string acoustic guitar. The strings on a nylon string guitar are tied off rather than using bridge pins. Likewise, the headstock of a nylon string guitar is slotted and has rollers rather than posts.

Step 1: Connect the String to the Bridge

1. Loosen the string from the slotted rollers and then remove it from the bridge to remove the old string.

2. Thread one end of the new string through the bridge's hole, leaving about 12 inches sticking out the back of the hole.

3. Pass the short end of the string over the bridge and under the long part of the string to secure it. Then, on the bridge's top, pass the short end under, over, and under itself.

4. Pull the long end of the string with one hand while moving the knot with the other, removing excess slack and causing the knot to lie flat on the bridge.

Step 2: Attach the String to the Tuners

1. Thread the string through the tuning post's hole. Bring the string end back and over the roller towards you, then under itself and in front of the hole.

2. Wrap the short end under and over itself a couple of times.

3. Wind the peg so that the strings wrap around the loop you just made, pressing it against the post.

To tauten the string, turn the peg with one hand.

Chapter 4

Tuning the Guitar

You must tune the strings after you have fixed all of the strings on your guitar.

Tuning the strings is the process of increasing or decreasing the

tension to produce a specific note. A guitar can be tuned in a variety of ways. And in this chapter, we'll go over the various ways you can tune your guitar. It is up to you to decide which method feels more natural to you. Because each method has its own set of advantages and disadvantages. Your ears and eyes are the most important parts of tuning a guitar, so be aware of any slight change in pitch.

Acoustic Guitar Tuning Using the Fundamental Tuning Method

Relative tuning is another method of tuning the guitar. It is so named because it does not require any external reference to tune the guitar. While this is one of the most versatile methods, it is not recommended for beginners. To use this method effectively, you must first learn the sound of each string. This method would be difficult to use for a beginner with little to no experience with the sound of each string. This method will come in handy if you need to tune your guitar while performing in front of a crowd.

You can use your guitar to produce harmonious and sonorous tones as long as you tune it properly. When the sound produced by the strings of a guitar is related to one another, you know the strings are in tune. To tune the guitar using this method, choose a starting point, such as the first string. The tune that string to pitch if possible, then use that same string to begin tuning all the other strings relative to the first string you started with. Similarly, the 5th fret method can be used to determine whether two strings are in tune. Because each string is connected to the next, the sound of an opened string and the string above it on the 5th fret should sound similar. You'll understand more as we go along with this method. The following are the steps to tune your guitar using the basic tuning method:

1. Understand the Meaning of Each String

First, you must be able to recognize each string and its name. An acoustic guitar has six strings, as stated in previous chapters. In order of thickness, the strings are labeled E, A, D, G, B, and E. The fattest string is the first string, which is closest to the ceiling when the guitar is held in a playing position. The first string is known as the low E string. The A string is the second string, which is located next to the first string. Similarly, the third string is known as the D string, the fourth string as the G string, and the fifth string as the B string. Finally, the high E string refers to the thinnest string, which is closest to the floor when holding the guitar in a playing position.

2. Identify each string's tuning pegs

The next step is to figure out how to identify the peg for each string. Follow the string from the neck to the corresponding peg to ensure you're turning the correct peg for the string. Before you begin tuning, pluck the string a few times and turn the peg clockwise and anticlockwise to hear the string's pitch rise and fall.

3. Select the correct pitch for each string.

This is the point at which you should tune your guitar using the most difficult method.

Your ears must be well trained to detect when the string strikes the correct note. Pluck the string and make any necessary adjustments to the peg. If the string's pitch is higher than the pitch of the note to be played, turn the peg to loosen the string's tension. Similarly, if the string is too low, turn the peg to tighten it. Rep to this step for each of the guitar's six strings until you are satisfied with the sound of each string.

4. Match the sound of the strings immediately below with the 5th fret.

The 5th-fret method will be used to determine whether each string is properly tuned. When you play the 5th fret open, the string immediately below it sounds the same. The only exception is the B string, which must be held on the 4th fret of the G string to be tuned. In other words, when you pluck the low E or 1st string, it should sound similar to the string immediately below it, i.e., the B string on the 5th fret. Similarly, plucking the B string and holding the G string on the 4th fret should sound similar. Do this for all of the strings and adjust as needed.

5. Play a Few Notes

Finally, strum a few notes to make sure the intervals are correct. You can check the guitar's tuning by playing the C chord or any other first position chord.

Using a Chromatic Tuner to Tune Your Acoustic Guitar

A chromatic tuner is another all-too-common method for tuning the guitar. When you use a chromatic tuner, you can tune your guitar more precisely than when you use your ears. Furthermore, this is the method recommended for beginners and intermediate players who have not trained their ears to detect the sound of each string. The only disadvantage is that you must spend extra money to purchase a chromatic tuner to use this method, and it only comes in handy when you need to tune your guitar.

Aside from the accuracy in tuning that this method provides, they can also tune your guitar quickly. Newer models of these tuners, particularly those for guitar, can tell you which string you're playing as well as its current pitch. The chromatic tuner will indicate whether the string is too sharp (too high) or too flat (too low).

To use this step to tune your guitar, follow the steps below:

1. Start the Chromatic Tuner.

The first step in using this method is to activate the chromatic tuner. Place the tuner close to your guitar so that when you pluck the string, it can pick the correct pitch.

You can put the tuner on a table and place it near the sound box. Also, make sure the chromatic tuner is set to measure the correct instrument. The chromatic tuner isn't just for tuning guitars. Some tuners are so versatile that you can tune guitars, pianos, violins, and even woodwind instruments with them. Set the tuner to tune an acoustic guitar rather than bass or electric guitar.

2. Take a String

Pluck the first string firmly, beginning with the first. The pitch of the sounding string is read by the chromatic tuner as the string sounds. The name of the string you pluck will be displayed on the digital screen, along with information about whether the string is too flat or too sharp.

Depending on the type of chromatic tuner, most come with a graph-like display. As a result, you can tune your guitar in real-time.

3. Change the tuning of the string (down or up).

When you pluck the string and it reads too flat on the tuner, you need to tighten it up. Continue to pluck the string as the chromatic tuner reads the pitch as you tighten it.

Continue to tighten the string until you reach the midpoint between the flat and sharp areas. Similarly, if it reads too sharp, the string is too tight, and you should loosen it. Repeat for all of the strings on the guitar.

4. Play a Few Chords

Play a few chords on the guitar to ensure that it is properly tuned. Because they are simple and sound familiar, you can strum the C chord or any other first position chord. Tuning Your Acoustic Guitar in a Different Way

There are other ways to tune a guitar besides using your ears and a chromatic or electric tuner. These alternative methods of tuning a guitar are referred to as the alternative method. Another method of tuning a guitar is to tune it to a fixed source, which is usually another instrument, such as a piano or a pitch pipe. This tuning method is ideal for playing the guitar alongside another instrument. In other words, the guitar and the other instrument will be in sync. The following instructions will show you how to tune your guitar using a fixed reference.

• Making Use of a Piano

The piano is one of the most commonly used instruments for tuning other instruments. Because it holds pitch so well, people use the piano as a fixed source to tune other instruments. Depending on the circumstances, a piano is usually tuned once a year or twice a year.

Assuming you have a well-tuned piano or, even better, an electronic keyboard nearby, all you need to do is match the open string to the appropriate keys on the piano. Play the low E on the keyboard when you pluck the open low E string on the guitar. Then adjust the tuners until the low E string is in tune. Check that the next string on the guitar is tuned. Rep this procedure until all of the strings on the guitar are properly tuned.

• Making Use of a Pitch Pipe

Using a pitch pipe, you can easily tune your guitar without using a piano or an electric keyboard. When necessary, the pitch pipe can be used as a standard tuning reference. You can use a special pitch pipe as a guitarist to play only the notes of the open string of a guitar. One of the most significant advantages of using a pitch pipe to tune a guitar is the ability to hold it firmly in your mouth while blowing, freeing up your hands to properly tune the guitar. The disadvantage of using it is that it can take some time to get used to relating a wind-produced pitch to a struck-string pitch.

In other words, tuning a guitar with a pitch pipe will be difficult for beginners because it is a wind instrument and a guitar is a string instrument.

Chapter 5

Developing Fundamental Playing Strategies

In this chapter, we'll take things up a notch by going over some of the fundamentals of playing the guitar. Knowing how to play the guitar entails more than just knowing which guitar to buy or how to string and tune it. What makes you a great guitarist are things like how to hold the guitar, how to manipulate your left and right fingers to create something melodious, and so on.

In this chapter, we'll go over the fundamental skills you'll need. We will also discuss basic music deciphering skills to give you a better chance of playing your first chord.

Standing or sitting with the guitar?

One of the first things you should get used to before you start playing is your posture. Your posture has a significant impact on how well you play a musical instrument. When playing the guitar, you can choose between sitting and standing positions. Whatever position you choose will not affect the sound you produce, but it will affect how comfortable you can play. We cannot emphasize enough how important it is to take the position that is most comfortable for you to get the best sound possible. You don't want to be struggling with your posture while also trying to navigate between chords and strumming patterns.

Many people prefer to sit when practicing because it allows them to concentrate better. However, when performing in public, many people prefer to stand to provide energy and vibe to the audience. The classical guitar, which normally requires you to sit, is the one exception that does not allow you to choose between standing and sitting. This is not to say that you can't play classical music while standing, but a more serious pursuit of classical-style guitar playing necessitates sitting. Don't let a bad position limit your potential. Here are some important things to remember when standing or sitting while playing the guitar. • Seated Position

Practicing how to play the guitar while seated allows you to maximize your practice time by practicing more efficiently and precisely. In addition, sitting allows you to overcome challenges such as restricted range of hand movement, sloppy playing, and hand tension. Sitting while playing the guitar improves accuracy and stamina, even when playing at a high speed/tempo. Assuming you are right-handed, the proper way to hold the guitar is to rest the waist on your right leg.

Furthermore, by lightly resting your right arm on the bass bout, make sure your feet are slightly apart to give the guitar a good balance. Supporting the neck of the guitar with your left hand only restricts your hand's ability to move freely. You should also balance the guitar so that you can remove your left hand from the fretboard without it falling over. As you sit in the chair, keep your back straight and your shoulders relaxed. Even if you can maintain a straight back, avoid leaning back into the chair. Finally, you can sit in front of a mirror to check your posture.

• Position of Standing

You can also play the guitar while standing. To play the guitar in this position, you must strap it to your shoulder for balance. When you fasten the strap to the pin on the guitar, you can stand upright to avoid tension while playing, allowing your arms to move freely and allowing you to play many octaves with precision. While playing the guitar while strapped to your shoulder is cool and gives you a Rockstar vibe, you must securely adjust the strap to a comfortable playing height.

Playing the guitar with a strap that is too high or too low will severely limit your ability to play. As a result, adjust the guitar so that it hangs high enough to allow your hand to move freely. The neck of the guitar should be included upward at a 30-degree angle when strapped around your shoulder. You can strap the guitar lower if you want, but if you do, place your left leg on a box during a passage to allow you to extend your playing hand and easily access more octaves.

Hands Positioning

You may already know this, but when playing the guitar, your left hand is your fretting hand and your right hand is your strumming hand. It takes skill to efficiently manipulate your fingers to form chords and move from one string to another smoothly and precisely. You must also be musically inclined to understand the strumming patterns that are appropriate for the music you are playing. Here are some pointers to help you get started with proper hand positioning.

• Position of the Left Hand

As previously stated, the fretting or fingering hand is the left hand. Stretch out your left hand, make a loose fist, and place your thumb roughly between your second and first fingers to get a sense of how your left hand should hold the guitar. Keep in mind that all of your knuckles should be bent. When you hold the guitar neck, your hand should look like this. Your thumb glides to the back of the guitar's neck, similar to but not as rigid as making a fist.

Whether you're relaxed or worried, keep your finger knuckles bent.

Left-hand fretting necessitates physical strength. So, if you try to speed up, don't ignore the strength; it will only affect your sound.

It takes a long time to develop the strength of your left hand. It should be noted that taking shortcuts rarely works and may even worsen the situation in the long run. Playing the guitar regularly is the best way to improve your left-hand strength. The most important thing to remember is to maintain a good left-hand position that allows you to play naturally and comfortably. When your hand begins to ache or hurt, remember to take a break and rest. Resting for some time to allow the body to catch up is important for any activity involving muscle development.

• Position of the Right Hand

The right hand, on the other hand, is where the actual rhythm is produced on the guitar through strums. The best way to hold your guitar while strumming it, whether sitting or standing, is at a 60-

degree angle to the strings. When playing with a pick, this position gives you an advantage. However, if you were playing fingerstyle, you might want to turn your right hand more perpendicular to the string, bringing it as close to a 90-degree angle as possible. When playing an acoustic guitar, you can use a pick or your fingers to strum.

Making Pick

Use of a

Using a produces a sound you're pick powerful whether playing pop, jazz, blues, rock 'n' roll, or country. When playing songs that involve strumming or striking primarily chords, using a pick is often recommended. The pick is held between the index finger and thumb, with the tip protruding perpendicular to the thumb. When you strike the string, your middle, ring, and pinky fingers rest on the pickguard. You use your elbow and wrist to strike the string with the pick. The more vigorously you must strum, the more elbow you must use. While playing, try not to grip the pick too tightly. Picks are available in a variety of gauges (gauge indicates how stiff or thick the pick is). Thinner picks are easier for beginners to use than heavy-gauge picks, which are mostly used by pros.

Making Use of Your Fingers

You can also play the guitar with your right-hand fingers, particularly if you fingerpick rather than strum the strings. The thumb plays the bass or low E string while fingerpicking. Also, when fingerpicking, use the tips of your fingers to play the strings.

Place your hand over the sound hole, keeping your wrist stationary but not rigid. Maintaining a slight arch in your wrist so that your finger comes down more vertically on the string is also beneficial. When playing classical guitar, for example, you must keep your fingers almost perpendicular to each other to draw strongly against the string.

Recognizing Guitar Notation

Unlike other instruments, you do not need to be able to read music to play the guitar. Musicians have developed a more straightforward method of communicating fundamental concepts such as song structure, chord progression, chord construction, and rhythmic figures. Understanding this abbreviation for tablature, rhythm slashes, and chord diagrams put you on the fast track to playing the guitar in no time.

A Chord Chart

Reading a chord diagram for a guitar is much easier than reading music. All you need to know are the frets, strings, and where to place your fingers to form a chord. A chord is the sounding of three or more notes at the same time. The anatomy of a chord chart is shown below, followed by a description of what the various parts of the diagram mean:

The guitar fretboard is represented by a grid with vertical and horizontal lines. It is essentially the guitar's perspective as if you were standing on a chair and placing the guitar on the floor.

The frets are represented by the horizontal lines. The thick line at the top of the grid represents the nut of the guitar, where the fretboard ends.

In other words, the first fret is the second vertical line from the top.

The vertical lines represent the guitar strings. The high E or first string is represented by the vertical line on the far right, while the low E or sixth string is represented by the vertical line on the far left.

The grid's dots represent the notes that you fret.

Each dot on the dots has a number assigned to it. The number denotes which finger should be used to fret that note.

Because the guitar can only be fretted with four fingers, the index finger is 1, the middle finger is 2, the ring finger is 3, and the little/pinky finger is 4.

Finally, the O and X symbols above some strings indicate which strings should be left open or not played. The O symbol represents an open string, while the X symbol represents a string that is not picked or struck.

Rhythm Slashes

are slash marks used by musicians to indicate how to play a rhyme but not what to play. So, after you've decided on a chord to play, the slash mark instructs you on how to play it. Consider the illustration below.

The G chord, for example, with four slashes beneath it indicates that you should finger the G chord and strike it four times. Following that are the D and A chords, with four slashes beneath them. You must strike the D chord twice, then switch to the A chord and strike it twice more. You can easily tell when to change chords and how many times to strike the strings with the rhythmic slashes.

Tablature

Finally, let's look at tablature. Tablature is a notation system used to graphically represent the guitar's strings and frets. While a chord diagram shows you which finger to use and where it should be placed, tablature shows you how to play music over time. The image below depicts two staff, tablature, and standard music notation staff. The second staff reflects what is happening in the regular musical staff above it. Tablature, also known as guitar tab, does not show you what notes to play, such as Eb, F#, or C, but it does tell you which string to fret and where on the fretboard to fret that string.

The image below shows some sample notes and where to play them on the guitar. The first note to play, according to the treble clef, is the low E, which is marked as 0 on the guitar tab. In that case, the 0 indicates that the 6th string or low E is being played open. The F note on the tablature is next, which is played on the second fret with the index finger on the 6th string. The G note on the tablature is played on the third fret of the sixth string with the ring finger. The same method is used for all of the notes on the tablature.

What is a Chord?

After you've grasped the concepts described in the preceding section, your best bet is to jump in and play your first chord. Chords are the foundation of songs. You can make a song with the guitar by strumming chords. You can't just smack any group of notes; you have to play a group of notes that are organized in some meaningful way. To begin, you can use a simple chord like the C chord, which is particularly guitar-friendly.

When you get the hang of playing a chord, you'll notice that you can move multiple fingers into position at the same time. For the time being, place your fingers on the frets and strings one at a time. To properly hold a C chord, follow the steps below:

1. Press your index finger down firmly on the 2nd string, 1st fret. Apply sufficient pressure to keep your finger from moving away

from the string. The key to properly holding a string is to bring it closer to the fret.

2. With your middle finger, press the 4th string at the 2nd fret. At this point, your first and middle fingers should be on the second and fourth strings, respectively, with an unfretted string on the third string.

3. Finally, press your ring finger firmly down on the 5th string, 3rd fret. You may need to spread your hand a little more to ensure that your thumb is properly grasping the back of the neck.

To play the C chord, strum the strings. When holding the guitar strings, make sure to press down on the string with your fingertip. Maintain a firm grip on the strings while not relaxing your fingers.

You can check if you're holding all the strings correctly by selecting a single string. A buzzing sound indicates that you are either not holding the string properly or that one of your fingers is interfering with or resting on the string. You can eliminate the buzz by adjusting that finger without removing your fingers from the string, then strum the chord again to ensure you have it correct.

Chapter 6

The Fretboard

You must have learned something about the fretboard from the previous chapter. Understanding the fretboard is essential for understanding guitar chords and progressions.

Learning a few notes on the fretboard is essential for a beginner. However, learning all of the possible notes that can be formed on the fretboard is an entirely different ball game. Learning all of the notes on the fretboard is a difficult task, but it is well worth it in the end.

Knowing the fundamentals of the guitar makes the learning process much more manageable.

Identifying the Fretboard Notes

We have seven notes on the guitar and in western music in general, ranging from A to G. These notes can be sharp or flat depending on how they are counted. When ascending the scale, you frequently count the notes as sharp. If you go down the scale, it is always seen as flat. In some cases, a single note can be referred to as both a flat and a sharp. C#/Db, for example, denotes a C sharp or a D flat. You can play either of the notes and get the same result.

When you have a firm understanding of the fretboard notes, guitar playing becomes more interesting. A standard classical acoustic guitar has 19 frets, but some models have as many as 21 or even 24 frets. However, for this section, we will explain how the notes on the first 12 frets are formed to provide you with everything you need to advance your playing skills. Below is a picture that summarizes everything, and after looking at it, you'll understand why each note is named the way it is.

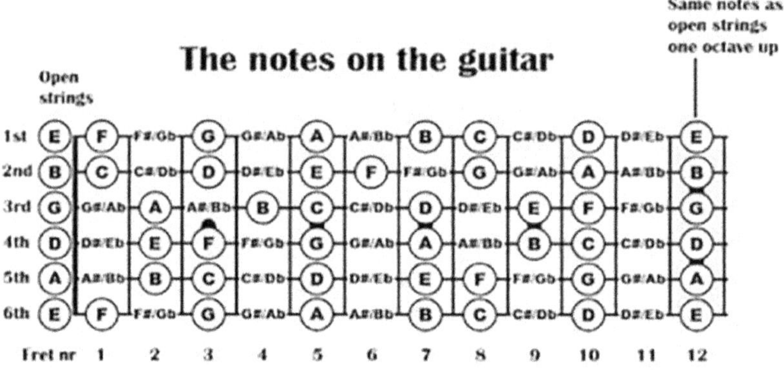

You might be wondering why the octave is on the 12th fret in the image above. The octave should be on the eighth fret, so why is it on the 12th? On the guitar, an octave is made up of eight naturals rather than eight notes spread out over eight notes. That means you won't be counting flats and sharps when counting the octave. Consider the first string: the first note is E,

followed by F, G, A, B, C, D, and E, for a total of eight notes that differ by an octave. In other words, it takes 12 frets on the guitar to get an octave higher than a specific note.

• First String

As you are aware, the first string is the thinnest string on the guitar. And, as you should know, the first string is the E string. When you play the first string without touching the fret, you'll get an E-note sound. Things change when you depress the first string on the first fret; you'll hear an F note.

You'd expect to hear an E# or Fb sound, but these notes don't exist, at least not on the guitar.

Moving to the next fret, depressing the 1st string on the second fret, and striking it will produce an F# or Gb note. We get an accidental note in this case that we didn't get in the first fret. This is due to the existence of the F#/Gb note. You guessed it: the G note is on the third fret. Because there is no H note in music, the fourth fret is an A.

As previously stated, you move from A to G and then back to A, repeating the cycle. Following the A on the fifth fret, there is an A# or Bb note on the sixth fret.

Take note that on the seventh fret, things get a little tricky again, as the note changed from B to C on the eighth fret.

This is because there can't be a B# or a Cb note. Following the C note on the seventh fret, the C# or Db note appears on the ninth fret.

The D note is on the tenth fret, and the D# or Eb note is on the eleventh fret. Finally, there's the E note on the twelfth fret. The open high E string is an octave higher than the E registered on the twelfth fret.

• Second String

As you already know, the second string is the next thinnest string or the B string. When you play the second string without holding anything on the fret, you will hear a B note, thus the name "B string." According to our explanation, moving from the first fret on the B string to the second fret should result in a sounding C rather than a B# or Cb note. As previously stated, the B# and Cb notes do not exist on the guitar. Because of the nature of the guitar's fret, which is a half-step apart, you would expect to encounter an accidental after every natural note, but there are none in the case of the B to C.

When we reach the third fret, depressing and striking it should result in a D note. Similarly, moving from the third to fourth fret will result in a D# or Eb note. And the E note will be on the fifth fret. Things change again when we move from the fifth fret to the sixth fret on the second string, as there are no accidentals between the E and F notes.

Moving from the sixth to the seventh fret produces an F# or Gb note. And, as you might expect, the note following the flat is natural; on the eighth fret, you'd get a G note. The G# or Ab note is on the ninth fret. Similarly, on the eleventh fret, we have the A# or Bb note, which brings us to the twelfth fret. The B note is an octave higher than the open B string on the twelfth fret.

• Third String

The third string, also known as the G string, is located directly above the second string. The method we used to count the notes on the first and second strings also applies to this string. In other words, the notes continue to vary from A to G, and no accidentals exist between B and C, as well as E and F. So, if you play the G string open without pressing anything on the fret, you should hear a G note, thus the string's name. However, pressing the third string on the first fret should produce a G# or Ab note.

With that established, the A note begins on the second fret, not the first fret, as you might have assumed because A comes after G. But, the next time, don't forget about the accidents. We have an A# or Bb note moving from the second to the third fret. The B note is on the fourth fret. However, there are no accidentals between the fourth and fifth frets.

In other words, we have a C note on the fifth fret rather than a B# or Cb note.

Furthermore, we have a C# or Db note on the sixth fret. And, as you might expect, the note on the seventh note is the note after the sixth fret with the flat, the D note. The note on the eighth fret is D# or Eb. And the E note is on the ninth fret. And, as luck would have it, there are no accidentals between the ninth and tenth frets as you move from E to F. The eleventh fret contains the F# or Gb note. Finally, on the twelfth fret, there is a G note that is an octave higher than the open G string.

• Fourth String

As you may know, the fourth string is also known as the D string, and it is a fairly thick string. It is situated between the G and A strings. The 4th string produces a D note sound when played without pressing any frets, hence the string's name. However, when you play a D# or Eb note on the first fret of the D string. Similarly, the flat's natural note on the first string is on the second fret of the fourth string.

To move from the second fret to the third fret, use the same method we used to name and count notes on the first string so far. Because there are no accidentals between these two notes on the fretboard, moving from an E note to an F note is always the same. Moving on, the F# or Eb note is on the fourth fret. Following that, we have the G note on the fifth fret. Following the G note is the G# or Ab note on the sixth fret. The A note is on the seventh fret, and the A# or Bb note is on the eighth fret.

The B note is on the ninth fret. However, there are no accidentals between the ninth and tenth frets. Because there are no accidentals between these notes, moving from B will always result in a C note. So we have the C note on the tenth fret. Furthermore, we have the C# or Db note on the eleventh fret. Finally, the D note on the twelfth fret is an octave higher than the open D string.

• Fifth String

The fifth string, also known as the A string, is the second thickest string on the guitar. The sound produced when playing the fifth string without holding any fret is an A note, hence the name. However, if you press the fifth string on the first fret, you will get an A# or Bb note. The second fret then produces a B note sound.

As previously stated, the B note is supposed to be a B# or Cb note, but there is no such note on the guitar. Moving from the second to third frets results in a C note.

The C# or Db note on the fourth fret comes after the note on the third fret.

The D note is on the fifth fret. If a fret has a flat, the next fret is the natural fret of the flat. If the sixth fret has a D# or Eb note, you should be able to guess the next fret's note with ease.

You are correct if you believe the note on the seventh fret is the E note.

Because there is no accidental between the E and F notes, the note after the seventh fret is the F note on the eighth fret, following the same naming pattern. The F# or Gb note is on the ninth fret, while the G note is on the tenth fret. The G# or Ab note is on the eleventh fret, which leads us to the final note on the twelfth fret, which is the A note. The open A string is an octave higher than the A note.

• Sixth String

Finally, the 6th string, also known as the low E string on an acoustic guitar, is the thickest. The name comes from playing the 6th string open without pressing any frets, which produces a low E note.

Because it's an E string, it'll have the same naming pattern as the high E note, but we'd still like to walk you through it so you have a better understanding. We always have an F note after an E note, and it is never an accident. So we have the F note on the first fret.

The F# or Gb note is on the second fret. The G note is located on the third fret, which is the next fret. The G# or Ab note is on the fifth fret, and the A note is on the sixth fret.

Following that, we have the A# or Bb note on the sixth fret, and the B string on the seventh fret. There are no accidentals between the B and C notes, so pay attention to the movement from the seventh to the eighth fret. So we have the C note on the eighth fret.

Similarly, we have the C# or Db note on the ninth fret. Following that, we have the D note on the tenth fret. The D# or Eb note is on the eleventh fret. Finally, we have the low E note on the twelfth fret, which is an octave higher than the opened low E string.

To summarize,

when counting notes on a guitar fret, moving from B to C and E to F has no accidents, i.e., there can't be a flat or a sharp in between. With this in mind, you can easily master the notes of any fret. We have named the first twelve notes on the fretboard of all acoustic guitars; you can use the same naming technique to name the entire fretboard of your guitar. When you're finished, you can compare it to materials found online.

Chapter 7

Understanding Music Notation

_K_nowing the names of the strings on the fretboard is useful, but it is not enough to be a great guitarist. Because the guitar is a musical instrument, having a basic understanding of music notation is essential. Although note-reading music is not required for guitar playing, understanding music notation is beneficial. In this chapter, we'll go over everything you need to know about musical notation for guitarists. You should be able to read music quickly and easily by the end of this chapter. So, become acquainted with the written symbols and notation practices used in this book so that you can better understand the written exercises and pieces in this book.

Recognizing Music Notation

When you think of standard notation for a guitar, you think of the staff, clef, and notes, just like on the piano, flute, violin, and saxophone. So, to begin, let us begin with some symbol introduction. In the section that followed, we went over music notation in greater depth, focusing on three of the most important elements of music: pitch, duration, and expression/articulation.

The canvas of the Composer: Staff, Clef, Bar-Lines, and Metrics

Over a century, the system of writing music has evolved to include new and improved approaches. When musicians write music today, they don't just scribble it down on any old scrap of paper.

The blank canvas isn't empty. In other words, musicians compose music using a series of horizontal grids that contain notes and other musical symbols. Here's an example of music written by a canvas composer:

• Staff

Musical staff, in general, refers to a grid of five lines and four spaces.

In music, the staff is used to indicate different pitches. There are various types of staff, but the bass and treble staffs are the most common. However, in guitar playing, we will focus primarily on the treble staff because most notes on the guitar are high pitched and are located on the treble staff. As previously stated, a staff has five lines and four spaces, and each line and space is named according to the type of staff. The lines on a treble staff are labeled E, G, B, D, and F from the first to the fifth. And the first four spaces on a treble staff are labeled F, A, C, and E. Notes at the bottom of a treble staff are low pitched, while notes higher up the treble staff are higher pitched.

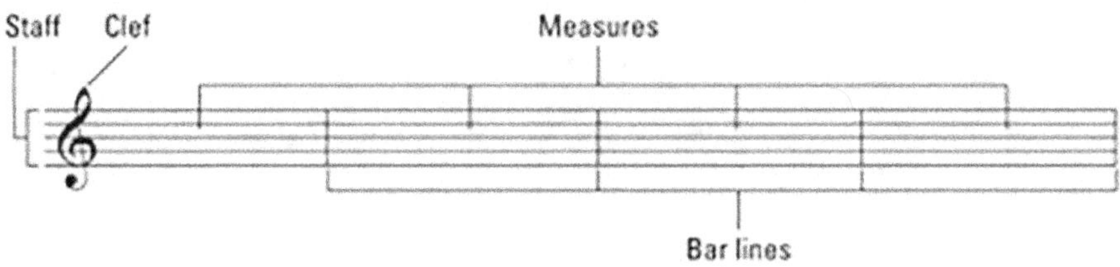

• Clef

The clef, like we have staff, determines what kind of staff we are dealing with. The clef is the first symbol you'll notice at the start of every staff. The bass and treble clefs are the two most common types of clefs. As previously stated, the guitar employs the treble clef, also known as the G clef. The G clef is distinguished by its resemblance to the letter G and the curlicue symbol wrapped around the G line of the staff, which is the second line from the bottom.

These are the origins of the name.

• Measurements and a bar-line

Aside from the staff and clef we just discussed, you must also have some kind of context in which to place notes in time. Most music has a beat or pulse that provides a rhythmic unit for the notes to play off of. The beat is typically felt in groups of two, three, or even four. The staff represents this division by vertical lines that divide the music into measures or bars. A measure is a distance between two vertical lines, and the vertical lines themselves are known as bar lines.

By organizing the notes into a smaller unit that supports the natural emphasis of the beat, grouping music into measures makes it more manageable.

The Low and High Pitch

As previously stated, the pitch of a note indicates its highness or lowness. As a result, when writing music notation, notes are placed on different lines or spaces to represent different pitches. Examine the diagram below for a breakdown of the various symbols and definitions that can be used to describe different pitches in musical notation. The diagram below is labeled 1 through 4, so we'll take things numerically and give them their proper names.

• Note

As previously stated, notes are either placed on a line or in between the line and space. The pitch of a note is determined by where it is placed on the staff. Notes near the bottom of the staff usually have a lower pitch than those higher up. In other words, the first note on the diagram above is a G note, and the next one is an A note. Because the G note is placed lower than the A note, it is expected to have a lower pitch. From bottom to top, the names of the five staff lines are E, G, B, D, and F. In addition, the notes on the four spaces between the lines spell out the word face, as in F, A, C, and E.

• General Ledger Lines

The note can be placed above, below, or within the staff.

When a note extends beyond the width of the staff, it is written on ledger lines. Notes on ledger lines indicate whether the pitch is higher or lower than the staff. Consider ledger lines to be short or temporary staff lines. The same rules apply when naming notes on lines and spaces on the staff. Consider the first ledger line below the staff, which is named, and the first ledger line above the staff, which is A. You could verify it by counting the notes from the bottom E to the ledger line below it, or from the upper F note to the ledger line.

• Unforeseen occurrences

Accidentals, also known as flats, sharps, and naturals, can be found in almost any musical context. Accidentals are notes that exist outside of the key and are identified by their key signature. When you want to raise the pitch by a semitone, use a sharp.

Similarly, a flat is used to reduce the pitch by a semitone. When you want to cancel the effect of a sharp or flat, you use the natural accidental. In some cases, an accidental can cancel or reinstate a previous accidental.

• Important Signature

A key signature is when you see a flat or a sharp beginning of the staff immediately after the clef. A key signature specifies which notes to play as sharps or flats for an entire piece, or at least the major section unless otherwise specified. For example, in the diagram above, the key signature is sharp on the fifth line or F note, which means that any note placed on the fifth line must be played a half step higher. In other words, in the case of the diagram, the key signature sends a loud and clear message that all F's are sharp.

How Long Should You Hold a Note?

Now that we've covered the fundamentals of music notation, let's move on to durations. Durations are symbols in staff that indicate how long a note should be played in a beat.

In addition to using different pitches to create rhythm, note duration can also be used. Music is created by combining pitch and rhythm. Rest is another type of duration that denotes musical silence. Also, by adding a tie to a note, you can lengthen it, which connects one note to another of the same pitch. The diagram below depicts some of the most common symbols used to indicate duration and symbols in a musical excerpt.

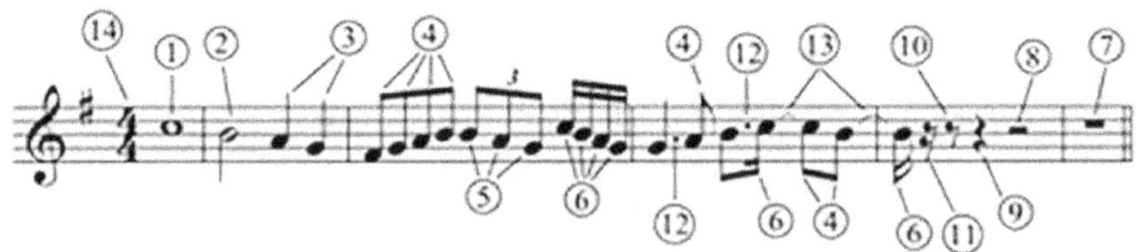

1. Overall Note

The whole note is a note that has four beats in 4/4 time or four crotchets. The entire note is the longest currently in use.

Other notes on the staff are fractions or multiples of whole notes.

2. A half-note

A half note, also known as a minim, is a note played twice as long as a whole note and with half the period. The half note in a note with a time signature of 4/4 is two beats long.

3. The Quarter Note

A quarter note, also known as a crochet note, is a note that is played one-quarter of the time it takes to play a whole note. Musicians frequently make the mistake of assuming that a quarter note equals one beat. But, in reality, a quarter note is not always a beat; it may or may not be a beat depending on the context.

4.Fourth Note

An eight note, also known as a quaver, is a note played for 1/8 the time it takes to play a whole note. A group of two or more eight notes on a scale can be beamed together. In this case, split the note appropriately while remaining within the time signature of the eight notes.

5.Five-Note Triplet

An eight-note triplet is a set of three notes played in the space of two eighth notes of the same rhythmic value.

6.Sixth Note

A sixteenth note, also known as a semiquaver, is a note on a musical staff that is played for half the duration of an eighth note. Two or more sixteenth notes can also be beamed together.

7. Complete Rest

A whole rest is a period of silence in the staff that is equal to one half of a breve rest or two half rests. A whole rest is four beats in a 4/4 time signature.

8. Half-Resting

In a 4/4 time signature, a half rest with a symbol shaped like a small rectangle sits on a staff line indicating two beats' rest.

9. Rest Period

A quarter rest is a period of silence equal to one-quarter note in length. In a 4/4 time signature, a quarter rest can last one beat. The quarter rest is a 14th of a beat. As a result, no note will be played for one beat.

10. rest

Eight rest, denoted by a symbol shaped like a middle-line note head that extends upward rather than downward, is used to denote a half beat's rest in 4/4.

11. Repose

The 16th rest is used to indicate a quarter beat's rest in 4/4, with a symbol shaped like a two-eight rest.

12. Enhancement

Augmentation is a dot-shaped symbol that appears to the right of a rest or a note head, indicating when to rest or increase the length of the note by half its original value. A quarter note, for example, is one beat, so a dotted quarter note is one and a half beats.

13. Tie

The tie represents a curved line connecting two notes of the same pitch. You play the first note for its full value, and instead of restriking the second (tied) note, you let it sustain for the sum of both notes' values.

14. Signature of Time

Finally, the time signature is a two-digit symbol that is usually found at the start of a stay. The time signature allows you to count the beats in a measure and determine which beat to emphasize or stress. A 4/4 time signature, for example, indicates that you should play four beats to the measure, with the quarter note receiving the beat or pulse.

Articulation and expression

Aside from the basic elements like pitch and duration, you will see other symbols in a written piece. Symbols for expression and articulation provide a variety of instructions, ranging from navigating instructions to repeating a specific passage and playing the music expressively. The diagram below describes some of these symbols:

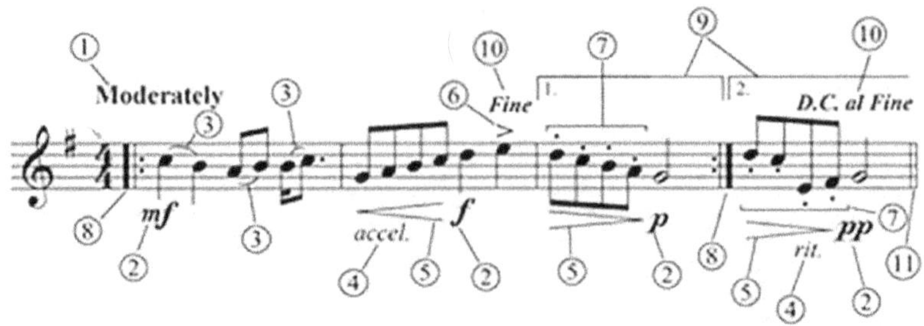

1. Tempo Direction

The symbol labeled 1 on the diagram represents the tempo heading, which is a word or phrase used to guide the speed or feel of a piece. The tempo heading is sometimes written in Italian, such as Adagio, Andante, and Moderato. In some cases, the tempo heading is written in the composer's native language, as in the diagram above, with the tempo heading "Moderately."

2. Dynamic Labeling

In the diagram above, the symbol labeled 2 represents the dynamic marking, which is a letter that indicates how soft or loud you should play. Similarly, the dynamic marking is frequently an abbreviation of Italian words such as mf for mezzo-forte, which means play medium loud. mp, p, f, ff, and pp are some other dynamic symbols.

3. Slur

The slur, denoted by the number 3 in the diagram above, is a curved line connecting two notes of different pitches. The slur instructs you to connect the second note to the first note smoothly. A slur is frequently seen in a piece that requires a legato approach, where the notes blend in an uninterrupted and sustained manner.

4. Ritardando and Accelerando

In the diagram, the symbol labeled 4 is abbreviated as accel. It is an accelerando that indicates how quickly you should play. It may be a written record in some cases. That is, ritardando will tell you how slow you should play.

5. Crescendo and Descendo

The crescendo, denoted by the number 5 in the diagram, is abbreviated as cresc. This symbol resembles an open wedge known as hairpins by one musician. The crescendo indicates how long you should play. The decrescendo or decresc. is used to indicate how soft you should play.

6. Accent

The accent symbol in the diagram is shaped like a small caret-like or wedge marking above or below a note, telling you to emphasize the note by striking it harder than usual.

7. Staccato

Dot In the diagram, the symbol labeled 7 represents a staccato dot, which is a small dot placed above or below the note head instructing you to play the note short and detached.

8. Repetition of Signs

The symbol labeled 8 in the diagram represents a repeat sign, which is a special bar-line type symbol used to indicate that the measures between the signs should be repeated.

9. Brackets at the end

The symbol 9 in the diagram represents the ending brackets, which are used to separate different endings in a repeated section. The diagram above's ending brackets indicate that you should play the measure under the first ending bracket the first time. On the repeat, you should only play the second ending bracket and skip the first ending bracket.

10 D.C. al Fine

In the diagram above, the symbol labeled 10 represents D.C. al fine, which is Italian for "from the top to the end." This symbol instructs you to return to the beginning and continue playing until you see the words, To Coda.

11. Bar-Line Double

Finally, symbol 11 in the diagram represents two bar lines that are closely spaced together, indicating the end of a section or if the line is a combination of a thick and thin pair of the end of a piece.

Chapter 8

Fundamental Major, Minor, and 7th Chords

So far, so good; we've made so much progress, and if you can keep up at this rate, you'll be ahead of the game before you know it. In this chapter, we'll go over some of the fundamental major, minor, and seventh chords you should know as a beginner. You can't learn all the chords all at once, but you can start somewhere. And we discovered that some chords are easier to learn than others, and they are used in our everyday songs. In other words, you can still play your favorite songs after learning this beginner's chord, which is one of the best ways to learn guitar chords.

We can't even begin to write about all of the possible chords on the guitar. If we cover every possible chord you can learn on the guitar, this book's pages will number in the thousands - not to exaggerate. In a nutshell, the following sections are a family of chords that you must know how to play as a beginner. They are fairly simple chords to learn to get you started on the right track.

The Fundamental Major and Minor Chords

1. A Chord from the A Family

To begin this section of the chapter, we'll look at family chords. Because they are relatively simple to play, family chords should be the first chords that every beginner learns. They have a lot of open strings, so you only have to press a few of them. Open position chords or open chords are chords with open strings. James Taylor's famous sound "Fire and Rain" is a perfect example of how the family chords were used. This family's basic chords are A, D, and E, and each chord in the A family is known as a major chord. Take note that in guitar, notes with no inscription beside them are always major chords.

Identifying the A Family Chord

Because this is the first chord you will hold on the guitar, we will show you how to do it. And the first thing to remember is to press the strings with the ball of your fingertip. Also, make certain that you press the string just behind the fret and make a note on the fret. Arrange your ginger so that the tip of your fingers is perpendicular to the neck. Also, keep your left-hand fingernails short so they don't get in the way of properly pressing the strings down. The diagrams below show the basic chords of the A family - A, D, and E chords on the guitar. Keep track of which strings you press and play. Strings marked with an X, such as the 6th string in the A chord and the 5th and 6th strings in the D chord, should not be played. Selectively stringing the guitar may appear awkward at first, but after a few attempts, it will feel quite natural.

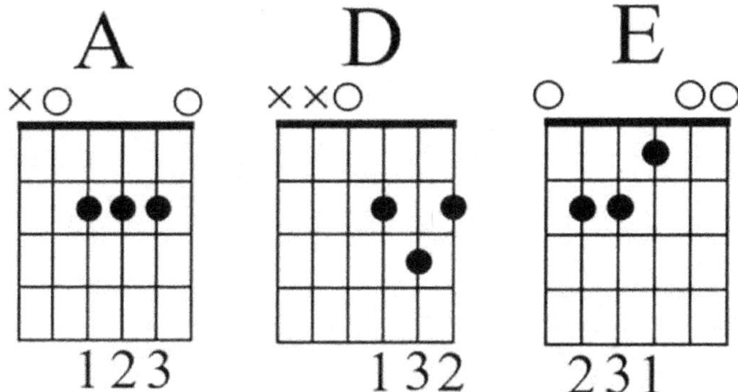

2. The Chord of the D Family

The D family chord is another basic chord you should learn as a beginner. This chord is made up of the D, Em, (E minor), G, and A chords. The D family chord includes two chords from the A family chord, the A and D chords, as well as two new chords, the Em and G chords. Because you already know how to play the A and D chords from the previous section, we'll concentrate on showing you how to play the new chords. Here Comes the Sun by the Beatles is a popular song in which you will hear the use of D family chords.

D Family Chord Fingering

On the guitar, the diagram below shows how to hold the Em and G chords in the D family. You may have noticed that none of the strings in the diagram below have an X symbol, indicating that you must strike all of the strings to get the full sound of the chord.

To hear the difference between major and minor chord qualities, play the E, the major chord described in the A family chords.

To play the E chord, simply press the third string on the first fret while holding the Em note. Strike the chord you're holding, then lift your finger on the third string and strike again to hear the difference in sound quality when switching from a major to a minor chord. The alternative fingering pattern for the G chord is also noteworthy.

The G chord can be held with 1-2-3 or 2-3-4 fingers. As a beginner, you should use the 1-2-3 configuration, but as you progress and your fingers gain strength and flexibility, you should switch to the 2-3-4 configuration. Why you might ask?

Because switching to other chords is easier and faster when using the 2-3-4 fingering for G.

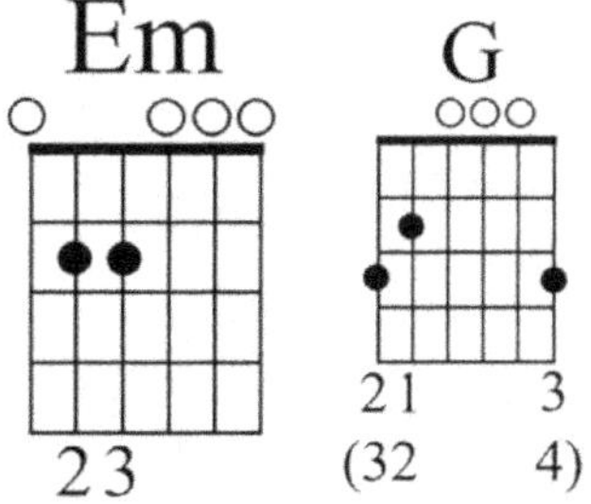

3. The Chord of the G Family

The G family chord is ideal for those who want to take things to the next level. G, Am, C, D, and Em chords make up the G family chord. And as you transfer your knowledge from one family to the next, you'll notice that we've already covered the D, Em, and G chords. As a result, we'll concentrate on the A minor and C chords in this chapter. If you're unsure about the sound of this family, listen to

James Taylor's popular song "You've Got a Friend" to hear the sound of a song that uses the G family chords.

G Family Chord Fingering

The fingering pattern for playing the Am and C chords is shown in the diagram below. It's worth noting that the finger patterns for these new chords in the G family are similar. Each chord is played with the index finger on the second string of the first fret. For both chords, the middle finger is holding the fourth string on the second fret. In other words, keeping both the index and middle fingers in place facilitates switching between the two chords.

Remember that switching chords are always easier when the fingering patterns are similar. When two or more notes in a chord sound the same, they are referred to as common tones. In each of the chords below, take note of the X over the 6th string. When strumming the Am or C chords, do not play the string.

4. The Chord of the C Family

Finally, in this chapter, we will go over the C family chords.

They are one of the beginner's chords to learn, despite being a little more technical to grasp. Some claim that C is the simplest key to play in. Furthermore, the C is sort of the starting point for everything in music. In reality, the C family contains far too many chords to master. C, Dm, Em, F, G, and Am are the basic chords that comprise the C family. However, if you practiced the A, D, and G family chords in the previous section, you should already know how to play the C, Em, and Am chords. So, in this section, we'll show you how to play the newer Dm and F chords. Kansas uses C family chords in "Dust in the Wind."

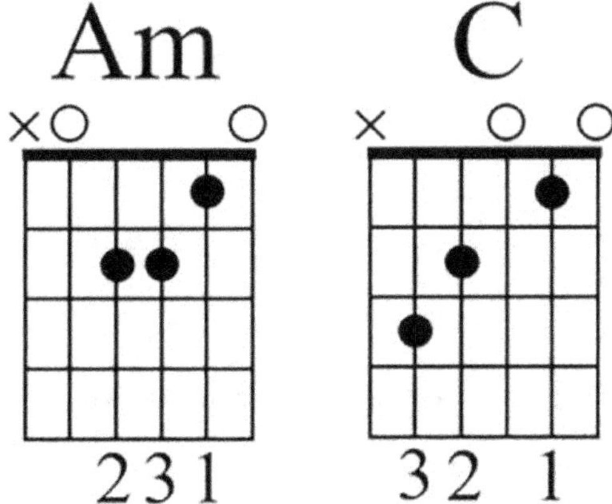

Identifying the C Family Chords

The diagram below shows that the second finger on the third string and second fret is used for both the Dm and F chords. As a result, holding down the common string makes switching between these two chords simple. Of all the basic chords, many people find the F chord to be the most difficult to play. This is due to the F's use of a barre. A barre is a chord formation scenario in which you use one finger to press down two or more strings at the same time. The barre, as in the F chord, is on the first fret of the first and second strings.

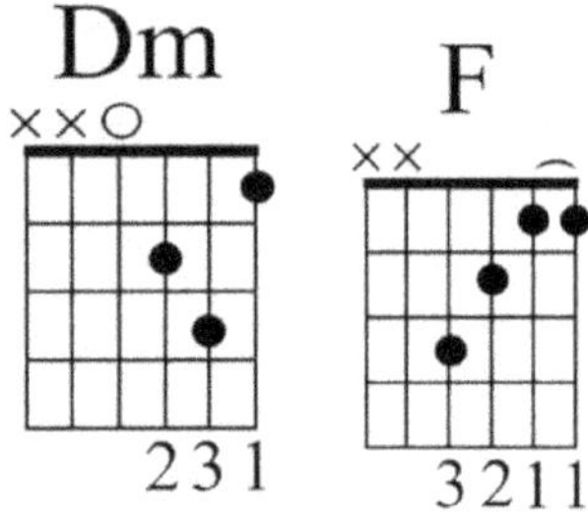

7th Chord Fundamentals

The basic 7th chords, also known as open position 7th chords, are as simple to play as simple minor or major chords.

Basic 7th chords, on the other hand, produce a more complex sound than basic minor and major chords. Players who have mastered the fundamental major and minor chords will appreciate the fundamental seventh chords even more. Furthermore, you must be well-trained to know where to substitute a regular major or minor chord for a 7th chord. Jazz music sounds jazzy with 7th chords, while blue music sounds blue with 7th chords.

There are various 7th chord variants with varying sound and quality. This section will concentrate on three of the most common and important types of 7th chords: dominant 7th, minor 7th, and major 7th.

1. 7th Chord Dominant

The 5th degree of a major scale is represented by the dominant 7th chord. When you talk about the C7 or any 7 chords, you're referring to the dominant 7th chord. It's worth noting that these notes are called the dominant 7th to distinguish them from other types of 7th chords like the minor 7th and major 7th. The dominant 7th chord was used to make popular sounds such as "I Saw Her Standing There" by the Beatles and "Wooly Bully" by Sam the Sham and the Pharaohs.

• The letters G7, D7, and C7

The G7, D7, and C7 chords are the first group of dominant 7th chords we'll look at. These are common open dominant 7th chords, as illustrated in the diagram below, and how to finger them on the guitar. If you already know how to play the C from the previous section, you can make the C7 by placing your pinky finger on the third string of the fourth fret. Take note of the Xs in the diagrams above the 5th and 6th strings on the D7 chord; try not to strum those strings. At the same time, don't strum the 6th string when playing C7 chords.

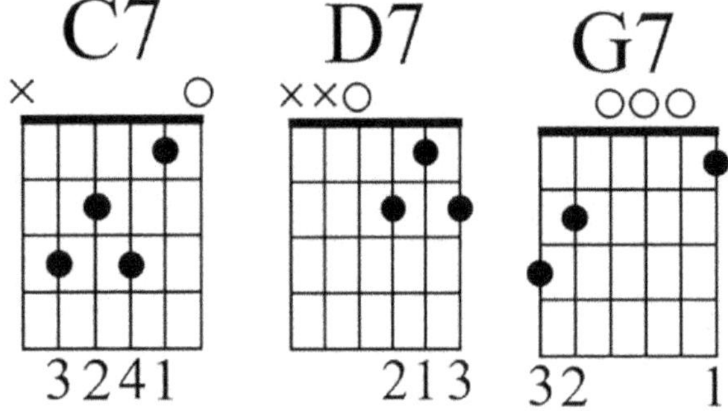

• E7 and A7

The E7 and A7 chords are two other common chords used to play songs based on dominant 7th chords. The diagram below demonstrates how to perform these chords. The E7 chord can be played easily from the E chord we discussed earlier. The E7 chord is formed by simply removing your third finger from the 4th string of the E chord. This section's version of E7 demonstrates how to use only two fingers. You can also play an open position with four fingers, which we'll go over in the next section. But for the time being, familiarize yourself with this version of E7 until you can fret it quickly. • E7 and B7 (Four-Finger Variant)

The E7 (four-finger variants) and B7 chords are the final two popular chords we'll look at in the dominant 7th chords. Many people believe that the four-finger version of the E7 sounds better than the two-finger version. Playing the E7 with four fingers is simple, especially if you already know how to play the E chord; simply place your pinky finger on the second string of the third fret. The B7 is frequently used in conjunction with the E7 to play certain songs in most songs.

Remember to avoid striking the sixth string on the B7 chord.

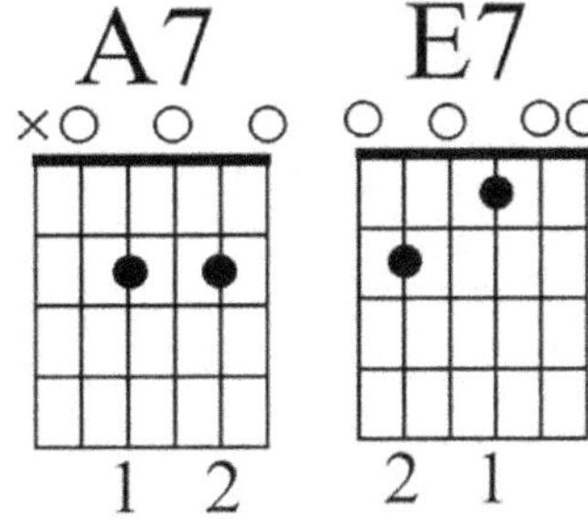

2. Dm7, Em7, and Am7 Minor 7th Chords

The minor 7th chords differ from the dominant 7th chords in that they have a softer character when played. The minor 7th chords are heard in the Doors' popular song "Light My Fire." The illustration below shows how to finger the three open positions of the minor 7th chords. It's worth noting that the Dm7 employs two-string barres. To play the Dm7 chord, you must press down two strings with a single finger (in this case, the first finger is used to press the first and second strings simultaneously at the first fret). The Dm7 note and the F chord share tones on the first and second fingers.

It allows you to slightly angle your finger or rotate it on its side to fret those barre notes when playing a barre chord. Hold the barre notes firmly to avoid any buzzes in the sound you produce as you play the chord. The fifth and sixth strings on the Dm7 chord have Xs above them, so don't strike them as you strum. The Am7 chord is fingered similarly to the C chord, with the exception that you must lift your third finger to play the Am7.

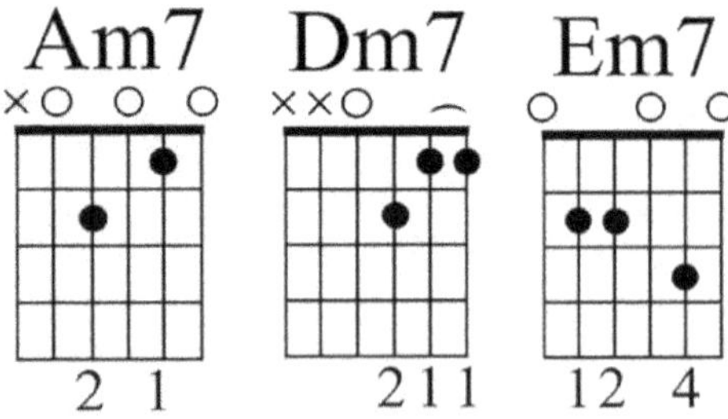

3. Cmaj7, Fmaj7, Amaj7, and Dmaj7 Major 7th Chords

Finally, let's look at the major 7th chords you should know as a beginner. Major 7th chords have a brighter sound than minor and dominant 7th chords. The popular song "Don't Let the Sun Catch You Crying" by Gerry and the Pacemakers use major 7th chords frequently. The diagram below shows how to finger the four major 7th chords in an open position on the guitar. Take note that the Dmaj7 has a three-string barre with the index finger on the second fret. The Dmaj7 chord is easier to play if you rotate your index finger to the side. When strumming the Dmaj7 and Fmaj7 chords, avoid playing the 6th and 5th strings marked X. Also, when strumming the Amaj7 and Cmaj7, do not play the 6th string marked X.

When switching from the Cmaj7 chord to the Fmaj7 chord, keep in mind that the middle and ring fingers move in a fixed shape across the strings. When playing the Cmaj7 chord, don't fret anything with your first finger; instead, keep it poised and curled above the 2nd string on the first fret so you can quickly bring it down for the switch to Fmaj7.

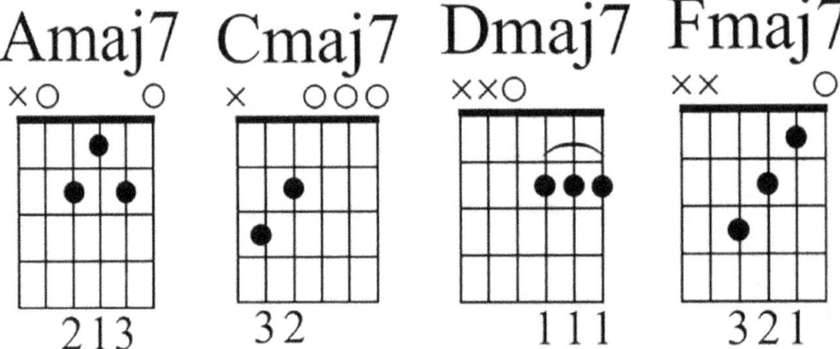

Chapter 9

Chord Technique

Chords, as you may be aware, are played with the left hand. So far, so good; we've covered a few of the fundamental chords you'll need to know as a beginner. So, in this chapter, we'll delve deeper into the world of chord formation on the guitar. The Nashville number system is our primary focus. You'll understand why chords are shaped the way they are if you understand the Nashville number system.

This chapter will show you how to create triad chords, 7th chords, 9th chords, 11th chords, and 13th chords, among other things. We will discuss the major, minor, diminished, and augmented chords in each of these sections. There are more complex chord formations that may appear out of this world, but we will leave that for you to figure out because we believe that by the end of this chapter, chord formation will be second nature to you. But, before we get into the

naming scheme, let's go over some fundamentals you should know before learning the Nashville number system.

Don't forget that you can help by learning more chords on your own once you've mastered the ones in this book.

Remember that there are numerous chords you can play on the guitar. So learning a few new chords won't hurt a fly. Also, for the time being, don't be too concerned with what your right hand is supposed to do. That will be determined in the following chapter, which will cover strumming patterns and everything your right hand should do.

The Fundamentals of Using the Nashville Number System in Chord Formation

The Nashville number system, as previously stated, is a method used by musicians to transcribe music by denoting the scale degree on which a chord is built. You can quickly figure out chord progressions using the Nashville number system. It is not difficult to comprehend. Rather than learning every single chord, you can use the Nashville number system to teach yourself new chords. The Nashville number system is popular because it allows for easy transposition of songs and changes the key of a sound without much difficulty. But, before we get into the meat of the Nashville system, consider these.

• **Roots** There is always a root note in every chord formation. The chord's name and key are frequently determined by the root note. For example, if the root note of a major chord is C, the chord formation key will be C major. Similarly, if the chord is a minor chord and the root note is A, the chord formation key is A minor. The first note in the chord is usually the root note in the Nashville number system.

• **Body** The body of a chord affects its function and sound. The body of a chord is affected by the type of chord you're playing, whether it's a major, minor, diminished, or augmented chord - they're all different.

• CAGED

Another critical concept to grasp is the CAGED guitar system. By revealing the relationship between a note and common open chord shapes, the CAGED system divides the fretboard into five sections. CAGED stands for C chord, A chord, G chord, E chord, and D chord. The diagram below shows how the CAGED system divides the fretboard.

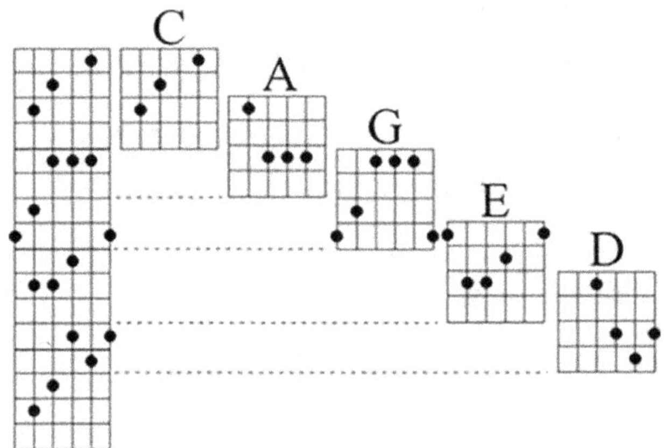

The Nashville Chord Formation Number System

See the table below for instructions on how to use the Nashville number system.

Key (1)	2	3	4	5	6	7
C	D	E	F	G	A	B
C#/Db	D#/Eb	F	F#/Gb	G#/Ab	A#/Bb	C
D	E	F#/Gb	G	A	B	C#/Db
D#/Eb	F	G	G#/Ab	A#/Bb	C	D
E	F#/Gb	G#/Ab	A	B	C#/Db	D#/Eb
F	G	A	A#/Bb	C	D	E
F#/Gb	G#/Ab	A#/Bb	B	C#/Db	D#/Eb	F
G	A	B	C	D	E	F#/Gb
G#/Ab	A#/Bb	C	C#/Db	D#/Eb	F	G
A	B	C#/Db	D	E	F#/Gb	G#/Ab
A#/Bb	C	D	D#/Eb	F	G	A
B	C#/Db	D#/Eb	E	F#/Gb	G#/Ab	A#/Bb

Chords in Major

As you may know, major chords are the most common type of chord in music. Major chords, as stated in previous chapters, are written as a single letter. However, in some cases, musicians use the uppercase letter "M" to represent major chords. Since we're interested in chord formation, let's look at how to use the Nashville numbering system to create triads, 7th, 9th, and 13 major chords.

• Chords of the Major Triad

A triad chord is a chord that consists of three notes. They are the most common chord type that beginners learn. A root chord is required to build a major triad chord. In this case, let's use C as the root chord. If C is the root chord, the following rules apply:

C- D- E- F- G- A

1 - 2 - 3 - 4 - 5 - 6

After you have numbered the scale, you must apply the formula. To create triad chords, use the following formula:

1 - 3 - 5

If you know the scale, you can use this formula to create any major triad chord. Let's take a closer look at the C major chord, for example. We can deduce that the C major triad chord will use C, E, and G notes using the formula and the C major scale from the table above. As a result, it is a C major chord if the strings on the guitar are in the configuration C, E, and G.

A diagram of C major chords is shown below.

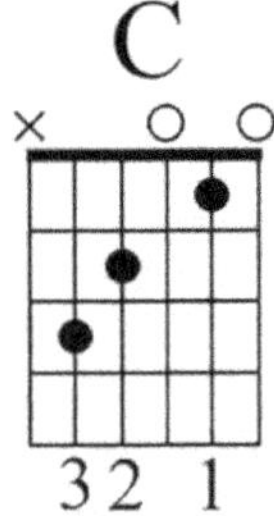

Other fingering patterns for the C chord can be found; the idea is that they will all have the same notes - C, E, and G.

You can use the same example with other chords, such as the G chord.

All G major chords should have notes G, B, and D, according to the table at the end of this chapter and the formula for constructing triad chords. Check with all of the G major notes you know. The same principle applies to all of the major scale's triad chords.

• 7th Major Chords

Four notes are required to build the major 7th chords. Let's use D as the root note to build a major 7th chord in this case. If D is the root note, the following rules apply:

D, E, F#/Gb, G, A, B, C#/Db, D

1 - 2 - 3 - 4 - 5 - 6 - 7 - 8

All you have to do with the number above is apply the formula for writing a major 7th chord to get the note needed to draw a D major 7th chord. 1 - 3 - 5 - 7 is the formula for constructing major 7th chords.

You can use this formula to create any note in the major 7th chord.

Applying the 1, 3, 5, and 7 analogy above yields notes D, F#/Gb, A, and C#/Db to draw a Dmaj7 chord. The diagram below depicts the D chord's configuration using the same D, F#/Gb, A, and C#/Db notes. Similarly, you can look for other D7 chord configurations; you'll notice that they all have the same fingering notes: D, F#/Gb, A, and C#/Db.

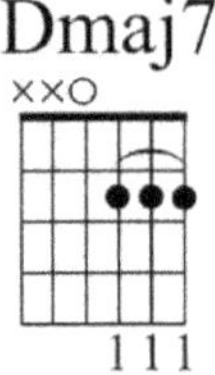

Similarly, you can experiment with major 7th chords such as the F. The notes for the F major 7th will be F, A, C, and E. To use another example, G major 7th will have the note configuration G, B, D, and F#/Gb. The idea is to stick to the formulas 1, 3, 5, and 7, and to always use the natural 7th note.

• 9th Major Chords

Things get a little more complicated when we start building major 9th chords. We usually stop at a 7 after determining the root note and writing out the scale for that note. For example, if we want to build C major 9th chords, which means C is the root note, we can do the following:

C – D – E – F – G – A – B – C – D – E

1 - 2 - 3 - 4 - 5 - 6 - 7 - 8 - 9 - 10

According to the analogy above, after the seventh note, we did not begin again at 1, but at an 8. In other words, 8 is also equivalent to 1, 9, is equivalent to 2, 10 is equivalent to 3, and so on. Major 9th chords are built using the following formula: 1 - 3 - 5 - 7 - 9

You can use this formula to create any major 9th chord. Because we're looking at the C chord, the C major 9th chords will have the notes C, E, G, B, and D. The diagram below depicts the fingering of the Cmaj9 chord; you can confirm the chord notes to see if they correspond to the notes we just deduced.

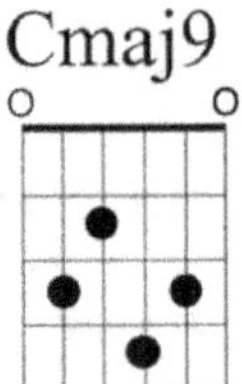

Aside from the diagram above, there are other Cmaj9 configurations to consider. Let's take a look at another example, the Fmaj9. The Fmaj9 chord will have the notes F, A, C, and E if the formula is followed. You can experiment with different major 9th chords and match the notes to the fingering pattern.

• Major Eleventh Chords

Major 11th chords are another type of major chord that you will encounter as you learn. These chords are more difficult to learn, but they will help you improve your playing skills. A root note is required to form any chord. After that, write down the scale and apply the formula. As an example, consider the C major 11th chord. Because C is the root chord, the following rules apply:

A - B - C - D - E - F - G - A - B - C - D - E - F - G - A - B - C - D - E - F - G

1 - 2 - 3 - 4 - 5 - 6 - 7 - 8 - 9 - 10 - 11 - 12

The analogy above shows that the number 8 is equivalent to another octave of the C scale. So we can read the 8 as a 1, the 9 as a 2, the 10 as a 3, and so on. We can write the C major 11th chord using that and the formula for constructing a major 11th chord. The following is the formula for writing a C major 11th chord:

1 - 3 - 5 - 7 - 9 - 11

We can deduce from this formula and the analogy above that the notes for a major 11th chord must be C, E, G, B, D, and F.

A C major 11th chord diagram is shown below. You can look for other examples of a C major 11th chord and compare the notes in the chord to the notes we just made.

Cmaj11

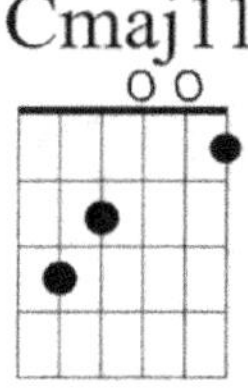

• 13th Major Chord

Finally, let's build a major 13th chord. We'll continue to build this chord with a C because it's the easiest to remember.

As you are aware, we must first identify the root note, which in this case is C. As a result, the following applies:

A - B - C - D - E - F - G - A - B - C - D - E - F - G - A - B - C - D - E - F - G

1 - 2 - 3 - 4 - 5 - 6 - 7 - 8 - 9 - 10 - 11 - 12

With that said, the next step is to take note of the formula for writing a major 13th chord and then apply it. A major 13th chord is written as follows: 1 - 3 - 5 - 7 - 9 - 11 - 13

Using this formula to create a C major 13th chord would result in the C, E, G, B, D, F, and A notes in the chord. However, because the guitar only has six strings, it is impossible to have seven notes on a chord. Certain notes, such as G, F, and D, are omitted in this case because they can be easily played on other instruments. As a result, the diagram of a C major 13th chord below makes sense.

Cmaj13

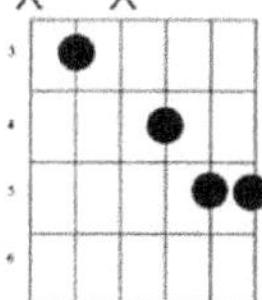

Chords in Minor

Minor chords, like major chords, are extremely common in guitar playing. In the same way that we have major triads, major 7ths, and so on, we also have minor chords. Here's how to build minor chords.

• Triad Chords in Minor

Minor triads are chords that contain three notes. A root chord is required to build a minor triad chord. Consider D to be the root chord. Let's start with the scale and number before we build the chord:

D, E, F#/Gb, G, A, B, C#/Db

1 - 2 - 3 - 4 - 5 - 6 - 7

Following the above, you'll need the formula for constructing a minor triad chord. A minor triad chord is composed as follows: 1 - 3b - 5

We can write the chord now that we have everything we need from the formula and scale. The notes in a D minor chord are D, F, and A. As you may have noticed, the third note was supposed to have an accidental, but the formula cancels it out, making it natural. A D minor chord is depicted below.

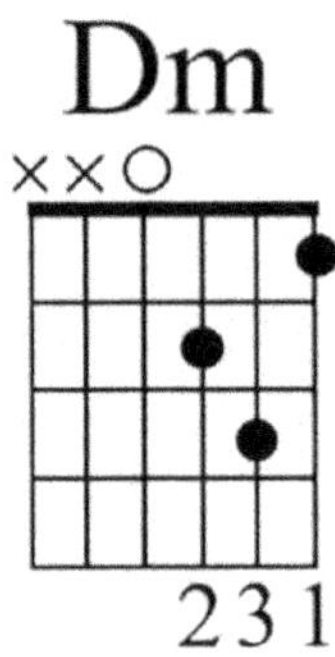

• 7th Minor Chords

The minor 7th chord is another type of minor chord that you will encounter while learning new chords on the guitar. Consider the D minor 7th chord as an example. The root note is a D because it is a D chord.

As a result, we will use a D scale, which means the following will apply:

G - A - B - C#/Db - D - E - F#/Gb - G - A - B - C#/Db - D - E - F#/Gb

1 - 2 - 3 - 4 - 5 - 6 - 7 - 8 - 9 - 10

All we need now is the formula for writing a minor 7th chord based on the number of the scale above. The following is the formula for writing a minor 7th chord:

1 - 3b - 5 - 7b

Using the analogy above, we can easily see that the notes in a D major 7th chord are D, F, A, and C. A D major 7th chord diagram is shown below.

In your spare time, you can look up other D major 7th chords and compare the notes.

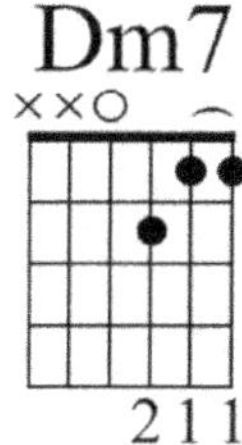

• 9th Minor Chords

The minor 9th chords are a little more difficult. Let's start with the simplest scale, the C scale. To write a C minor 9th chord, first, write out the C minor scale, number it, and then apply it to the minor 9th chord. A C minor chord is numbered as follows:

C – D – E – F – G – A – B – C – D – E

1 - 2 - 3 - 4 - 5 - 6 - 7 - 8 - 9 - 10

That being said, we now require the formula for writing a minor 9th chord. The following is the formula for writing a minor 9th chord:

1 - 3b - 5 - 7b - 9

Using this formula, we can determine that a C minor 9th chord has five notes: C, Eb, G, Bb, and D. The diagram of the C minor 9th chord below confirms that these notes are correct.

Cmin9

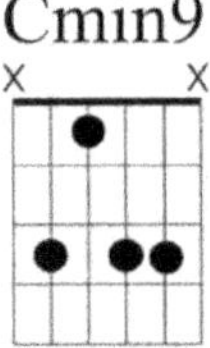

• 11th Minor Chords

Another type of minor chord we'll look at is the minor 11th chord. Consider the C minor 11th chord, for example. Because it is a C chord, C is the root note, so we will continue to use the C minor scale.

A - B - C - D - E - F - G - A - B - C - D - E - F - G - A - B - C - D - E - F - G

1 - 2 - 3 - 4 - 5 - 6 - 7 - 8 - 9 - 10 - 11 - 12

Based on the analogy above, all we need is the formula for writing a minor 11th chord to get started. The following is the formula for writing a minor 11th chord:

1 - 3b - 5 - 7b - 9 - 11

As a result, we can use this formula to determine that a C minor 11th chord has six notes: C, D#/Eb, G, A#/Bb, D, and F. The diagram below confirms the notes in a C minor 11th chord. You can also look at other notes.

Cmin11

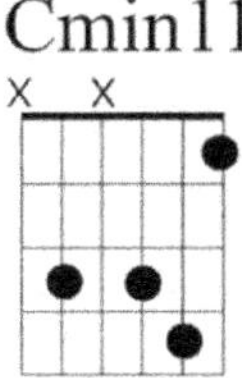

• 13th chords in minor

Finally, consider how minor 13th chords are constructed. Let us now examine how the C minor 13th note is formed. The root note should always be the first thing we notice. The root note, in this case, is C, and the following rules apply:

C - D - E - F - G - A - B - C - D - E - F - G - A - B - C - D - E - F - G - A - B

1 - 2 - 3 - 4 - 5 - 6 - 7 - 8 - 9 - 10 - 11 - 12 - 13 - 14

Following on from the preceding, we require the formula for writing minor 13th chords. The minor 13th chord formula is: 1 - 3b - 5 - 7b - 13

In other words, C, D#/Eb, G, A#/Bb, and A are the notes in a C minor 13th chord. You can use the diagram of a C minor 13th chord below to confirm the notes.

Cmin13

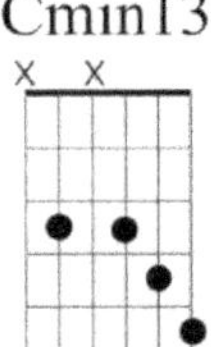

Other Complex Chord Formation

On the guitar, there are more than just major and minor chords. The fundamentals of forming any guitar chord are to first identify the root chord, then devise the scale and write it using the Nashville number system. Apply the chord formula to get the chord notes, and you're done. Consider this section to be a kind of practical section in which you must apply yourself. We will only introduce you to the formula for these new chord types and provide one or two examples. What you must do is comprehend the formula and draw the chord yourself. You can also try these chords with any scale you want as long as you follow the instructions.

Dominant Chords

We will be discussing four different types of dominant chords in this article:

1. Dominant 7th chords: These chords are written as 1 - 3 - 5 - 7b. Examples include G7, C7, and A7, among others.

2. Dominant 9th chords: These chords are written as 1 - 3 - 5 - 7b - 9. C9, D9, G9, and E9 are common examples.

3. Dominant 11th chords: These chords are written as 1 - 3 - 5 - 7b - 9 - 11. C11, D11, and other common examples

4. Dominant 13th chords: These chords are written as 1 - 3 - 5 - 7b - 9 - 11 - 13. C13 and D13 are two common examples.

Chords should be added.

We will be discussing two types of add chords in this article:

1. Add 9th chords: The chords are written as 1 - 3 - 5 - 9. Cadd9 and Eadd9 are two common examples.

2. Add 11th chords: 1 - 3 - 5 - 11 is the formula for writing these chords. Cadd11, Eadd9, and other common examples

Chords for Sus

We will be discussing two types of Sus chords in this article:

1. Sus2 chords: These chords are written using the formula 1 - 2 - 5. Csus2, Esus2, and other common examples

2. Sus4 chords: These chords are written using the formula 1 - 4 - 5. Csus4, Esus4, and other common examples

Chord Changes

We will be discussing four different types of altered chords here:

1. Dominant 7th sharp 9th chords: These chords are written as

1 - 3 - 5 - 7b - 9#. G7#9, E7#9, and other common examples

2. Dominant 7th flat 9th chords: These chords are written as 1 - 3 - 5 - 7b - 9b. C7b9, D7b9, and other common examples

3. Dominant 7th sharp 5th chords: These chords are written as 1 - 3 - 5 - 7b - 5#. C7#5, A7#5, and other common examples

4. Dominant 7th flat 5th chords: These chords are written as 1 - 3 - 5 - 7b - 5b. C7b5, A7b5, and other common examples

Reduced Chords

There are two types of diminished chords that we will discuss here:

1. Diminished chords: The formula for writing these chords is 1 - 3b - 5b. Bdim, Ddim, and other common examples

2. Diminished 7th chords: These chords are written as 1 - 3b - 5b - 7bb. Cdim7, Adim7, and other common examples

Chord Extensions

Finally, there are two types of augmented chords that we will discuss here:

1. Augmented chords: These chords are written as 1 - 3 - 5#. Caug, Aug, and other common examples

7th augmented chords: These chords are written using the formula 1 - 3 - 5# - 7b. Caug7, Aaug7, and other common examples

Chapter 10

Rhythm Techniques

So far, so good; we've talked about chords on the guitar in general. So, by now, you should have a good understanding of what chords are, what notes are, and how to combine notes to form a chord. This section will be more focused on the topic of rhythm. The action of striking strings on the guitar produces rhythm with the right hand. The way you strike the string has the most influence on your rhythm. While we advise every beginner to strum the guitar in a way that feels natural to the song, there are other ways to strum the guitar. To begin, especially in classical music, you can create a rhythm with the guitar by picking the strings individually rather than striking them all at once. Furthermore, if you prefer rock and roll music, there are other strumming patterns you can try, such as striking all the strings with upward and downward strokes. This chapter will cover all of these topics and more. But first, let us define what strumming is and the various patterns.

Using Your Right Hand to Strumming

Strumming is the act of dragging a pick (or your fingers) across the guitar strings. To play the chords you fingered on the fretboard with your left hand, drag the pick or your finger downwards. However, by doing so, you create rhythm. For example, if all you do is stick to a tempo, pick-drag in a regular pattern, or stroke, say, one stroke per beat, you are strumming the guitar in rhythm. In reality, whether you do it intentionally or unintentionally, that is all there is to music. To be more specific, you can strum the rhythm of a quarter-note, which is appropriate for some music, such as the Beatles' "Let It Be" or other ballads. Strumming one bar of a quarter E note looks like the notation in the diagram below, which uses rhythm slashes rather than note heads to tell you to strike the enter chord.

One of the most difficult aspects of learning to play the guitar is remaining aware of the rhythm while performing all of the repetitions.

Strumming a guitar entails more than just striking the strings. You must be consistent in your practice, have the skill, and have a good understanding of musicianship to be able to come up with a cool lick or riff on the guitar.

The concept of developing a good rhythm begins with learning how to play consistently for some time, after which you can deviate from the strumming pattern into something you create. The main goal is to create something tasteful, appropriate, and not overly numerous.

• Backstrokes

Downstrokes are represented on the staff by a symbol that looks like an "n." Downstrokes are strumming motions that involve dragging the pick or finger across the guitar's multiple strings. Downstrokes are among the first types of strumming patterns to learn on a guitar as a beginner because they are simple and easy to wrap your fingers around. Before switching from one chord to another, keep your downstrokes consistent. When playing downstrokes, you can strike all of the strikes at once, as in strumming, or you can pluck a string or a couple of strings at a time, as in fingerpicking.

• Eight-Note Downstroke Strumming

To get the most out of strumming strings, shift your focus from the plodding rhythms of a quarter-note strumming pattern to eighth notes. In mathematics, an eight-note has one-twelfth the value of a quarter note, but in music, an eight-note is twice as fast, precise, and frequent. So, instead of playing one strum to the beat, you can play two. In other words, you'll have to strike the strings twice per beat, which will require you to move your hand twice as fast. Your hands will only move once per beat if it's a quarter note.

At a much slower and more moderate tempo, you can easily perform downstrokes on eight notes, but at a faster tempo, you may have to alternate strumming an eight-note with upstrokes and downstrokes.

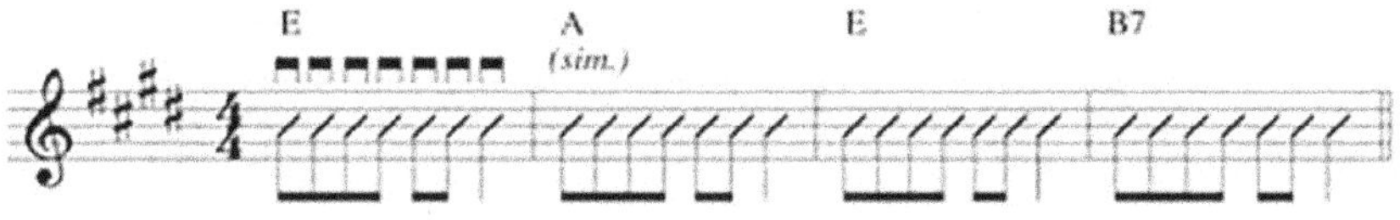

143

The diagram below shows some chords as well as how to use the eight-note strumming pattern for the first three beats of each bar and a quarter for the last beat of each bar. The quarter note at the end of each bar and the start of a new bar gives you a little more time to switch from one chord to another. The term sim. appears in the diagram; it is a music notation that tells you to continue similarly. Sim is a notation for the direction of articulation, such as upstrokes and downstrokes.

• Eight-Note Downstrokes Reading

Instead of the usual slashed, we use slashes with stems (vertical lines drawn from the note heads) and beams (horizontal lines connecting the stems). Eight notes, for example, have stems and beams connecting them, whereas quarter notes have a single stem attached to each of them. An eight-note on its own has a small flag rather than a beam.

So, even though this newly introduced notation explains specific rhythmic values such as eighth notes and quarter notes, the note heads are still angled and elongated, rather than the rounded, smaller note heads used to indicate individual pitches.

• Strong upward strokes

Upstrokes are represented on the staff by a symbol that looks like a "v," and they produce the opposite sound as downstrokes.

The upstroke is when you drag your fingers or pick them up from the floor to the ceiling across the strings. Playing upstrokes may appear less natural than playing downstrokes at first, but you will quickly get the hang of it. Another reason why the upstroke does not feel natural to beginners is that they are going against gravity. Some beginners struggle with properly holding the pick, which occasionally gets stuck between the strings.

Upstrokes are especially useful when playing eight-note upbeats as the strokes in between the quarter note beats. Remember, when you first start playing, don't worry too much about hitting all of the strings on your upstroke. When playing an E chord with an upstroke, for example, you don't have to strike all six strings down to the low E. In general, the first three or four strings from the bottom string or high E string should always be your target strings.

Another thing to keep in mind about upstrokes is that they are not given the same amount of time as downstrokes. Most of the time, you only use the upstroke in conjunction with the downstroke. While you can use downstrokes on their own and they will sound fine throughout the song. It is uncommon to see upstrokes used alone or without being surrounded by downstrokes.

• Using Strum to Mix Single Notes

Apart from simultaneously strumming multiple strings on the guitar, there are numerous other ways to add rhythm to what you're playing. A guitarist does not have to strike all of the strings every time, just as a pianist does not always plunk down all of his/her fingers at one to play a chord. To play something rhythmical, a guitarist can pick down single notes on the guitar.

• Strum the Pick

This method is similar to the piano-plunking counterpart. You can add rhythm to your guitar playing by plucking individual strings rather than strumming them. A pick-strum pattern is when you separate a chord into individual notes and play them, possibly the chord's base notes.

It is a great way to add more rhythm variety to a chord to separate the treble and bass notes and play them independently in time. It even improves your chordal textures. As a guitarist, you can even arrange an interplay of the various parts, such as treble and bass complementarity or counterpart.

• Boom Chick's

The boom chick pattern is another simple way to achieve rhythm in your guitar playing. This pattern is very efficient, and you do not have to play all of the chord notes at once. As a result, you can play the bass note on the boom while the rest of the notes are played on the chick.

Chapter 11

Using the Pentatonic Scale and Riffs to Add Melody

At this point in the book, with all of the information absorbed, you should be able to play along with certain songs. Although playing alone does not necessarily imply that you are an expert, you are better off than when you first began. All that remains for us to do now is provide you with some helpful hints to help you make the most of everything you now know. As a result, we will introduce you to the pentatonic scale and riffs in this chapter.

Almost everything in this book up to this point has taught you how to hold a chord, how they are constructed, how to strum, and so on. But we haven't yet discussed combining chords to create something melodious.

As a result, in this chapter, we'll talk about using the pentatonic scale and riffs to add melody to songs.

Pentatonic Scale

The minor and major scales are the most commonly used in guitar playing and music in general. When you're looking for something more melodic, scales like the pentatonic scales come into play. The pentatonic scale is more than just a scale; it is widely used to help students learn chord progressions. The scale's beauty is how it sounds over every chord change in a key. You can start making music almost immediately by changing and following the chord progression on the pentatonic scale.

5th fret   8th fret

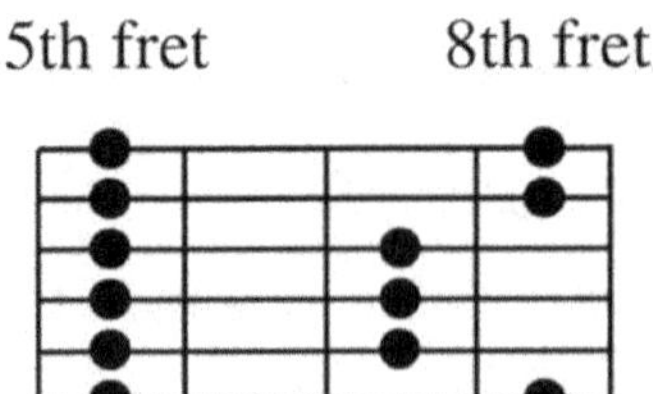

The pentatonic scale has five notes, as the name implies, and differs from the normal seven-note minor and major scales by two notes. As a result, the missing notes produce a sound that is less linear and more open than either the minor or major scale. Furthermore, the pentatonic scale is more ambiguous, which is a good thing because you will rarely hear a bad note. When we say bad notes, we mean notes that are within the key but do not fit well with the rest of the notes. In reality, the importance of the pentatonic scale cannot be overstated.

The diagram above depicts the neck outline of a 5th position pentatonic scale form. The first string is the topmost line, just like in a tab staff. This is a tab staff containing the notes you can play on the pentatonic scale, not a chord. The notes on the fifth fret of the tab staff are all played with your left index finger. Notes on the seventh fret are played with the ring finger, while notes on the eighth fret are played with the pinky or little finger. The middle finger does not play at all on this staff.

Three Ways to Solo on the Pentatonic Scale

This section will show you how to play a single pentatonic scale pattern in three different musical settings. As a beginner, you should know this trick by heart because you can use it as a shortcut or quick mental calculation to wail away to a minor-key, major-key, or blues song. The pentatonic scale can help you quickly create good-sounding music. As we progress through the pentatonic scale, you'll see why the notes work the way they do.

Playing the pentatonic scale is simple once you know which finger goes where. To begin, place your index finger on the fifth fret of the first string with your left hand. Relax your hand so that your other fingers don't get in the way of your playing while hovering above the sixth, seventh, and eighth frets. You are in the fifth position and ready to play in this situation. You can experiment by going from bottom to top and playing each note individually. Remember to use upstrokes and downstrokes with this scale until you feel natural using it while moving your lefthand finger comfortably.

The table below shows the C pentatonic major scale in eighth notes. This pentatonic pattern places your left hand in a stationary position, allowing your fingers to easily reach their respective frets without any left-hand movement or stretching.

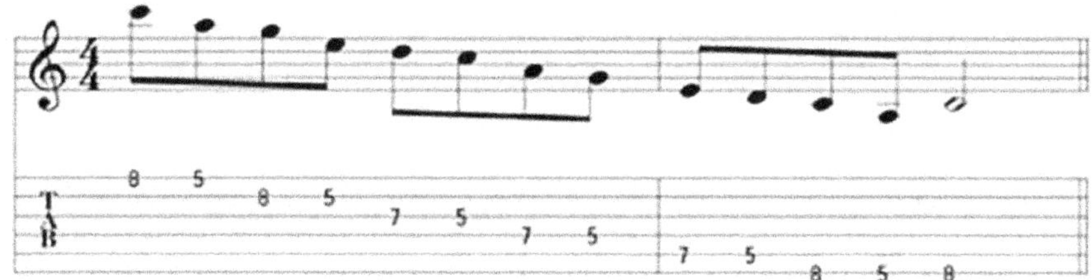

1. A Major Key Progression

It's time to look at the pentatonic scale as it progresses through a major key. A written solo in C major in a 4/4 medium tempo grove is included below. The solo is a mixture of eighth notes and quarter notes made up primarily of notes from the C major pentatonic scale, moving down and up the neck as soon as you get a sense of how the notes sound, keep practicing until you can move from one note to the next as smoothly as possible.

2. A Minor Key Progression

Another example of the pentatonic scale in action, this time in the minor key. For those looking for something completely different, here is a written piece in the key of A minor. When the feel changes to a heavy backbeat 4/4, the sounds change dramatically.

• Riffing on Riffs

Riffs, on the other hand, are another component of rock and roll songs that serve as the perfect bridge between the melodic phrase and the chord progression. In this section, we'll delve deep into the world of riffing and discover why riffs are such essential and inseparable components of rock and roll.

• Fundamental Riffs

Let's start with the fundamental riff, which makes use of your guitar's lower register. When playing riffs, keep in mind that you should only strike one string at a time, but your pick strokes should have the same power as when playing chords. Even if the riff sounds familiar, it is critical to executing the articulation and rhythm of the written piece as precisely as possible. Make certain that your ears do not gloss over the tricky parts.

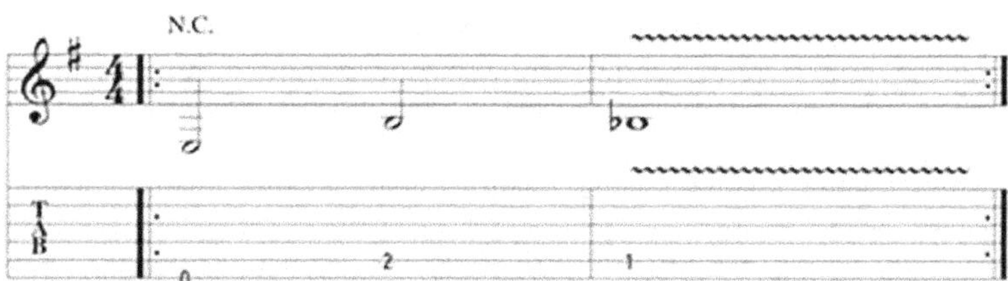

• Riffs on half and whole notes

The first thing you should know about riffs is that they don't have to be flashy to be memorable. To create an eerie, menacing effect, the sheet below uses only whole notes and half notes.

When writing a piece, you can add life to fretted notes with long values (whole notes and half notes) by vibrating them with your left hand. To add vibrato, quickly pull and release the string (causing a slight bend in the string) to cause the note to waver. Vibrato in guitar playing allows you to add intensity to slower notes. A wavy line placed above the note indicates that vibrato should be used.

• Riffs on the eighth and quarter notes

The non-syncopated rhythmic unit of quarter eight and quarter notes is another simple way to play riffs other than slow riffs created from whole notes and half notes. Here are two sheets of riffs that combine quarter and eighth notes. So, pay attention to the pick strike indicated for downstrokes and upstrokes.

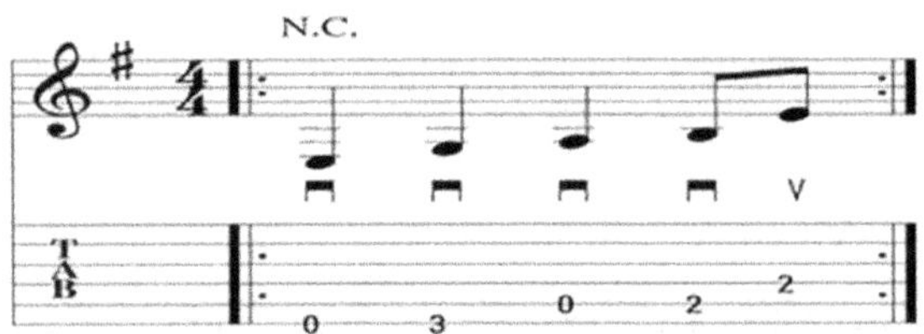

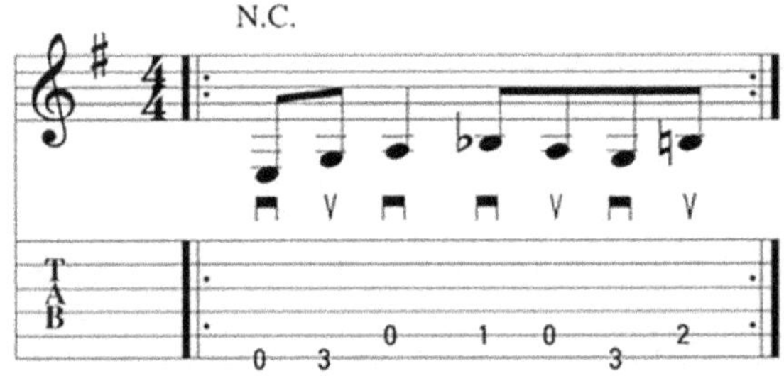

Did you notice the F# in the key signature of both of the above-written pieces? That is, all of the Fs in the written piece are sharped, and the key is neither E minor nor G major. Even if the two riffs don't contain any Fs, we can tell they're in E minor because the riff revolves around the root note E.

Now, in the next written piece below, let us try out the boogie riff. This boogie riff is mostly quarter notes with a couple of shuffle eighth notes thrown in to give the groove some extra oomph. The tempo in the piece is fairly fast, so be careful to execute the long-short rhythm of the shuffle eighth notes correctly.

A riff comprised of eighth notes creates a sense of continuous motion and is excellent for propelling a song forward. The piece below is in all eighth notes. Take note of how easily the end of the first measure flows into the start of the second to create a seamless sound. Take note of the D# and Bb, which are two chromatic, or out of key, notes in E minor.

While the previous piece was a simple one-bar riff repeated over and over, the following piece is long and steady with an eight-note phrase that goes for two measures before repeating. Because riffs are self-contained and brief, they can be easily repeated back to back and looped without interruption. All of the riffs we've looked at so far can be played seamlessly, and we encourage you to practice multiple times until you can play the riff flawlessly, both rhythmically and technically.

The following piece is a two-bar riff in steady eighth notes. You can experiment with it by going from one end of the riff to the other.

Remember that maintaining a consistent and steady delivery over two bars is one thing, but staying solid over bars upon bars or minutes upon minutes of playing the same riff within a groove is quite another.

• Riffs on the 16th Note

Finally, let's look at 16th note riffs, which don't have to be syncopated or fast just because they have 16th notes. The piece below is a riff that you can use to practice your speed because it starts with quarter notes, then eighth notes, and finally sixteenth notes.

Much heavy metal and rock riffs, including the infamous gallop pattern, are based on 16th notes. The following piece is a galloping riff that you can try out on your own.

T hen again, a riff written in 16th notes may be as fast as it can be, as in the case of the hard-rock grooves in the piece below. Keep an eye out for the alternate picking indications in this example.

Chapter 12

Songwriting and Music

t this point, we'd like to express our congratulations. Because if you've followed all of the steps we've outlined so far, you should be able to play a written piece with ease. As a result, in this chapter, we'll walk you through some songs and how they're played. Don't worry, we won't be going through the entire song, just a portion of it. By the way, we'll be discussing songs that use the chords we covered in this chapter. In other words, you shouldn't have any trouble remembering or switching between chords.

So, without further ado, let's dive right in.

Kumbaya

The first song on our list is Kumbaya, the ultimate campfire song.

Although the song's origins are unknown, it is an African American spiritual song. Kumbaya, which means "come by here," is sung throughout the islands, from the south to the north. You must be familiar with the chords A, E, and D to play this song. Strumming can be kept simple by using downstrokes throughout the piece. Finally, knowing how to make a campfire with two sticks, some dry leaves, and a magnifying glass is required to play this song perfectly.

Below is the sheet music for the song Kumbaya, which contains all of the information you'll need, but here are a few pointers to keep in mind. When playing Kumbaya, keep in mind that the pickup measure is referred to as the first measure. And, as we all know, the first measure of a song frequently begins with a couple of missing beats. In the case of Kumbaya, the first two beats are missing. Take note that there should be a musical silence or rest in the pickup measure. Play nothing during the musical silence.

Take note that the last bar in this piece is missing two beats - beat 3 and beat 4. As a result, the missing beats in the last measure are what allow you to repeat the pickup measure so you can play the song over and over again. The missing meat allows the measure to be combined with the first incomplete one to create the required total of four beats.

Kumbaya

Sweet Chariot, swing low!

Another song we'll look at in this chapter is the all-time favorite Swing Low, Sweet Chariot. This is an African American spiritual song about the Prophet Elijah being transported to heaven in a chariot. It was written by Wallis Willis, a Choctaw freedman. To play this song on the guitar, you must be familiar with the D, Em, G, and A chords. You'd also need to have practiced your downstrokes and upstrokes to be able to play this piece and sing like James Earl Jones.

Swing Low, Sweet Chariot begins with a single beat pickup and a beat rest. The time signature to play on in the sheet below is 4/4. You'll also notice that beat 2 of measures 2, 4, and 6 have two strums rather than one. So, when you get to those notes, beat a downstroke and an upstroke twice as fast as a regular strum. Don't forget about the two sharp key signatures on C and F notes, which means that any note on the C or F line on the staff will be sharp.

This is a very simple piece to comprehend. Once you've figured out how the rhythm works, the rest is simple.

Play around with this piece until it is as smooth as possible. Your primary focus should be on transitioning between chords, so you don't have to pause abruptly every time you want to change chords.

The Auld Lang Syne

Following that, we'll look at yet another fantastic piece of music from Auld Lang Syne. This composition is based on a Scottish poem written by Robert Burns in the late 1780s. The tune of Auld Lang Syne was adapted from the traditional folk song "Roud." This piece was used in many countries to bid farewell to the old years at the stroke of midnight on New Year's Eve. You must be able to play the chords Em, D, C, Am, and G to play this piece. You must also be able to play down and down-up strums on the guitar for the rhythm.

This piece is a little longer than the others we've treated so far, so it may require a little more attention and time to get your head around. But one thing is certain: you can play this piece on the guitar because you have been taught everything you need to know about playing it. Measure 8 in this piece, on the other hand, is a little tricky because you'll have to play three different chords in that same measure. In measure 8, you must play the D, Am, and Em all at the same time.

When you get to the second half of the measure, you'll have to change chords on each beat, i.e., one strike per chord. Begin by playing measure 8 slowly and repeatedly. And before you know it, you'll be able to play the entire song effortlessly. Take note that when switching from G to C (bars 4-6 and 12-19), fingering G with fingers 2, 3, and 4 instead of 1, 2, and 3 facilitates the chord change. The third and second fingers combine to form a shape that moves only one string.

Row the Boat Ashore, Michael

Another song you can play using basic major and minor chords is Michael, Row the Boat Ashore, an African-American spiritual song first recorded at St. Helena Island during the American Civil War. The Highwaymen, a U.S. bank, released the best-known recording of this folk music in 1960. This song is now sung all over the world. You must be able to play the chords G, F, Em, Dm, and C, as well as a syncopated eighth-note strum, to play this song.

Before you begin, take your time to read through the sheet and understand the time signature, strumming pattern, and every other piece of information embedded in it.

You'd need to be familiar with downstrokes and upstrokes, as well as a sim, for this sheet. This song's strumming pattern is syncopated. As a result, the strum that usually occurs on beat 3 arrives half a beat early. This strumming pattern lends the song a Latin flavor. When

Michael, Row the Boat Ashore

playing this song, keep in mind the 4/4 time signature.

The House on the Range

So far, so good; we've looked at a few songs that can be played with the basic major and minor chords. Let's take a look at some songs that use some seventh chords. The sheet music for Home on the Range sometimes referred to as the unofficial anthem of the American West, is provided below. Although it is a bit long, this song is fairly simple and uses chords that you are already familiar with. You must be familiar with the chords G7, D7, F, C7, and C to play this song. You should also be able to play a bass strum pattern and, for fun, how to wail like a coyote.

The sheet has a few interesting features, particularly the strumming pattern. In the sheet, instead of simply strumming the chord for three beats, your bass strum over the rhythm slashes, playing only the lowest notes of the chords beginning with the first beat and then strumming the remaining notes of the chord on the second and third beats. The sim in this sheet indicates that you should continue to play this pattern throughout the sheet.

All During the Night

Finally, let's look at another song that uses seventh chords that you can play. All Through the Night was originally recorded by Jules Shear. This is a mid-tempo folk-rock song that you can groove to when you want to hear something sleepy. You must be able to play the chords A7, E7, G, and D to play this song.

You must also be able to repeat signs. Use the two-finger variant for the E7 in this

track; it makes switching between chords easier.

The repeat signs (two dots that look like a colon) in the sheet below indicate that you will play a specific measure twice. As a result, you must play measures 1, 2, 3, 4, and then 1, 2, 3, and 5 twice.

All Through the Night

Chapter 13

Ten Common Guitar Mistakes to Avoid

Finally, in this chapter, we'll go over how to improve your playing abilities. Because we have practically taught you everything you need to know as a beginner at this point. All you have to do now is practice, practice, and practice some more. And remember to try something new every time you practice. To be honest, learning the guitar is a huge undertaking that requires a lot of time and patience. Furthermore, as you learn, you may make one or more errors. So we wrote this chapter to educate you on some common bad habits you may be developing as you learn. It is preferable to learn how to play the guitar correctly from the start rather than having to correct bad habits as you progress. With that said, here are ten mistakes you should avoid.

1. Excessive Effort in Play

While it takes a lot of energy to hold the chord firmly, your fingers must be flexible. It may take some practice for you to get your hands around holding strings firmly while remaining flexible enough to switch between notes easily. When holding notes, many beginners make the mistake of stiffening their fingers far too much. After playing the note, they find it difficult to quickly switch to another note without pausing. This pause to change notes will affect your sound and make what you're playing unappealing. The worst part is that exerting too much effort with your fingers will result in early fatigue. You may even begin to feel pains much sooner than you should, limiting the amount of time you can practice and thus slowing your overall progress.

2. Practicing on a Low-Quality Guitar

Another thing to keep in mind is that you should not get a professional guitar setup. Much of what we just said about putting in too much effort to play boils down to finding a good, easy-to-play instrument. When you buy a non-professional guitar, you may believe you have to put in a lot of effort to get the strings to sound right. A low-quality guitar frequently has higher string actions that require more effort to press the string. Even if the difference between the string and the fretboard is only a few millimeters, it will be felt by the fingers. The main advantage of a professional guitar is the lower string action.

Not to mention the sounds of the low-quality guitar, which are frequently off. Don't let the price of a guitar push you to buy one you'll later regret or one that will make learning difficult for you.

3. Learning Too Quickly

While you may want to go as fast as you can to demonstrate your skill as a guitarist, it's okay to take things slowly as a beginner. It's okay if you can't follow a song at 100% speed as a beginner after learning the notes you'll use to play it. Instead, try to slow the song down to about 50% of its original speed to allow you to switch between chords. Because switching chords is one of the most difficult things for a beginner. And you must understand that it is acceptable to be slow when switching between chords; your speed will eventually improve. What matters is that you keep at it, stay consistent, and you'll notice a gradual increase in your playing speed. Make the rookie mistake of attempting to practice fast-paced songs. Choose songs with a slower tempo. It's also critical to avoid sloppy practices when switching chords.

4. Not Practicing with a Metronome

We just discussed taking things slowly; to do so properly, you'll need a metronome. A metronome is a versatile tool that is useful when practicing a song. The metronome assists you in three major ways: To begin with, you can use it to slow down your practice. Second, the metronome can be used to develop a natural sense of rhyme. Finally, you can use the metronome to get a good sense of the progression you're working on. It's undeniably easier to practice at a slower pace, but most people start slowly and then unknowingly speed up later on.

This is common when practicing without a metronome. However, practicing with a metronome counteracts this effect by providing a clear indicator to follow. Because the metronome will alert you if you slow down or speed up too much.

5. Practicing Too Many Effects

While adding vibrato, riffs, and reverb to whatever song you're playing may sound great, too much of it is always bad. We're not trying to discourage you or say you shouldn't practice with effects; on the contrary, effects can help you cover up sloppy techniques and mistakes; however, keep your use of effects to a minimum. You can divide your practice session into two sessions, one for practicing with effects and the other for practicing without effects. This way, you'll be able to evaluate your techniques without being obscured by a wall of sound

6. Unreliable Practice

One major bad habit you should avoid is not practicing consistently. Once a month practice will have little to no effect on your playing ability. Set aside a specific time of day and days of the week to practice if you truly want to learn how to play the guitar. The more you practice, the more muscle memory you develop. Guitar practice necessitates a wide range of complex motor skills. Consistent repetition, which comes down to practice, is the best way to make these movements appear effortless and natural. It is preferable to practice for one hour every day rather than for ten hours on a single day. Consistency is the key to muscle memory.

7. Ignoring Music Theory

As a beginner, you should not consider learning music theory to be too difficult. Although music theory can appear to be quite technical at first glance, it is not, especially when you take the time to understand it. They are, in fact, quite fascinating. Understanding music theory expands your knowledge of how to best combine chords and transition from one key to another, among many other benefits. Without a doubt, learning music theory takes time; however, it is well worth every second of your time. You'll be memorizing scale shapes and chord progressions if you don't have a strong foundation in music theory. Consider it a formula for improving your guitar understanding without having to memorize so much.

8. Attempting to learn too many things at once

While we've taught you a lot in this book, it's best not to consume it all at once. Take your time digesting them one at a time. It doesn't matter how much time you spend getting acquainted with and mastering a specific lesson; what matters is that you can do it. But don't misinterpret this to mean that being highly motivated to learn more is a bad thing. The problem is that you are moving on to learn something new before you have even mastered the song you were previously learning. Learning all of the modes in all 12 keys and all of the scale shapes is a fantastic goal, especially if you are willing to work hard and be disciplined enough to learn them all. However, it is preferable to specialize in one or two areas rather than being mediocre at everything.

9. Ignorance of other musical genres

You might not notice this mistake right away, but limiting yourself to one music genre isn't a good way to learn. Although learning to play a genre of music you enjoy can help make learning more enjoyable, don't limit yourself to just one. Every piece of music has something to teach you about playing. Furthermore, once you start listening to other music genres, you'll be surprised at how much inspiration you'll get from different chord combinations and rhythms. For example, if you listen to a lot of rock music, you'll be familiar with strumming patterns, but when you start listening to blues and classical music, you'll learn more about fingerpicking.

10. Occupation with Perfection

Finally, getting too caught up in perfection is a common mistake made by many beginners, especially in the early stages of practice.

Everyone sounds different and unique because we all have quirks. So, rather than striving for perfection, it's okay to have a little quirk in your sound. So, don't be alarmed or disappointed if you notice an irregularity in your sound as you learn. This isn't to say you shouldn't try your hardest to practice perfectly to achieve the best results in perfect technique. We're trying to say that when you're performing, you should focus on getting everything as perfect as possible and learn to turn off your inner critic and just play.

Conclusion

To summarize, while learning new things on the guitar can help you improve your playing, practice is the key to becoming an expert. As we have been emphasizing, you must be consistent in your practice. And, if you truly want to enjoy learning the guitar, it is always a good idea to spend some money on a high-quality instrument. You won't have to work as hard to get the best sound out of a high-quality guitar. As a result, your fingers will be less sore, allowing you to play for longer periods.

We've discussed how to buy a guitar. Use the information provided as a guide to educate yourself on what to look for when purchasing the best guitar. Remember not to get too caught up in the price of a guitar. While you may have a budget, your goal should be to get the best guitar you can afford, not the cheapest guitar you can find. After purchasing a guitar, make certain that you string it with the appropriate string for you. Plus, tuning the guitar can be a pain, but we discussed different ways to tune the guitar, so you can use whichever one you feel most comfortable with.

Take note of the basic playing strategies we discussed, such as learning the beginner's chord first before progressing to the more technical ones later on. Your main challenge as a beginner learning to play the guitar may be switching between chords. Do not be disheartened if you are experiencing this difficulty. Beginners frequently struggle with switching between chords. It is beneficial to begin as slowly as is comfortable for you. Consistent practice will help you improve your speed.

Playing along with your favorite songs is the best way to learn how to play the guitar. You won't have any trouble coping with the rhythm because you know the song. Most importantly, you only need to know the chord progression and possibly the strumming pattern to be able to play any song. Practicing your favorite song makes learning the guitar more enjoyable.

www.ingramcontent.com/pod-product-compliance
Lightning Source LLC
LaVergne TN
LVHW041315200726
843509LV00009B/503